Education 5.0 to Mobilise Social, Scientific and Technological Entrepreneurship – Educación 5.0 para Movilizar Emprendimiento Social, Científico y Tecnológico

Future of Education – Futuro de la Educación

Eds. María Soledad Ramírez-Montoya, Rasikh Tariq, Leonardo David Glasserman Morales,
Edgar Omar López-Caudana & Inés Alvarez-Icaza Longoria

VOL. 2

María Soledad Ramírez-Montoya, Edgar Omar López-Caudana,
Inés Alvarez-Icaza Longoria, Carlos Enrique George Reyes,
Paloma Suárez Brito & Pamela Geraldine Olivo Montaño

Education 5.0 to Mobilise Social, Scientific and Technological Entrepreneurship – Educación 5.0 para Movilizar Emprendimiento Social, Científico y Tecnológico

OpenEdR4C Platform – Plataforma OpenEdR4C

PETER LANG

Berlin · Bruxelles · Chennai · Lausanne · New York · Oxford

Bibliographic Information published by the Deutsche Nationalbibliothek
The Deutsche Nationalbibliothek lists this publication in the Deutsche Nationalbibliografie; detailed bibliographic data is available online at http://dnb.d-nb.de.

Library of Congress Cataloging-in-Publication Data
A CIP catalog record for this book has been applied for at the Library of Congress.

Cover Credit: Michael Haderer, Vienna, Austria

ISSN 3053-4593 (Print) | 3053-4607 (Online)
ISBN 978-3-631-93304-6 (Print)
ISBN 978-3-631-93316-9 (ePDF)
ISBN 978-3-631-93317-6 (ePUB)
DOI 10.3726/b23401

info@peterlang.com

Published by Peter Lang GmbH, Berlin, Germany

This publication has been peer reviewed.

www.peterlang.com

Contact for General Product Safety Regulation (GPSR): gpsr@peterlang.com

Table of Contents

ENGLISH

Education 5.0 to Mobilise Social, Scientific and Technological Entrepreneurship

OpenEdR4C Platform

María Soledad Ramírez-Montoya

(PhD in Philosophy and Educational Sciences)

Inés Alvarez Icaza Longoria

(PhD in Engineering)

Edgar Omar López Caudana

(PhD in Communications and Electronics)

Carlos Enrique George Reyes

(Doctor in Educational Sciences)

Paloma Suárez Brito

(PhD in Psychology)

Pamela Geraldine Olivo Montaño

(Ph.D. in Philosophy of Science)

Figure 1.
IRG-R4C Researchers mobiliser of the OpenEdR4C platform

About Us

We are members of the IRG-R4C Interdisciplinary Research Group Scaling Complex Thinking for All (Figure 1). We are passionate about taking higher education to new levels of excellence. We are dedicated to developing and promoting advanced reasoning competencies to face the complexity of the modern world. We use Open Science strategies and the most advanced 5.0 technologies, such as artificial intelligence and data science, to create training systems that prepare people for the challenges of the future. Our work is linked to projects that integrate universities, industries, the government and the civil sector, always seeking sustainable solutions that benefit the whole of society.

Our vision is clear and ambitious: to contribute meaningfully to the future of education, creating innovative solutions to the problems and challenges of today's society. We align with the goals of UNESCO's 2030 Agenda for Sustainable Development, fostering interdisciplinary collaboration and building robust academic networks. At IRG-R4C, we work to train a new generation of highly competitive professionals committed to social welfare who always seek to enable innovative solutions that respond to present and future challenges.

Editorial Letter

We started an exciting project to develop, experiment on and implement an OpenEDR4C online educational platform characterised by functions and services based on artificial intelligence and interactive and gamified multimedia interfaces powered by 5.0 technologies. This platform, called Education 5.0, seeks to promote scientific, technological and social entrepreneurship through training in complex thinking skills for higher education students and people in continuous learning.

Our goal in the project OpenEdR4C: Education Platform 5.0 to strengthen Scientific, Technological and Social Entrepreneurship through scaling Complex Thinking Competences, is for beneficiaries to participate in active learning dynamics in complex real-world environments, thus promoting the creation of technological solutions for priority problems in specific contexts. The platform is theoretically based on complex thinking, whose objective is to promote the development of high skills and offer training scenarios linked to the real world as well as resources for innovation, education and open science.

The benefit will not only be for students who make use of the platform but also for people from academia and decision-makers in various institutions. We collaborate with technology companies, ministries of education and labour, universities, NGOs and society at large to promote lifelong learning and universal access to knowledge. This project is crucial because various studies have shown that stimulating and scaling complex thinking in people influences the analysis, identification and evaluation of complex systems, generating new knowledge and promoting the development of entrepreneurial products and processes.

Let's come together to seize this opportunity and promote social, scientific and technological entrepreneurship, building a future full of innovation and continuous learning together!

OBJECTIVES

Our goal is to mobilise an online educational platform that benefits from the use of Technologies 5.0 and increases analysis and proposals from complex thinking and entrepreneurship. This platform is designed to improve performance in complex thinking competencies in higher education students and people in continuous learning. Using training scenarios, technological tools and modular activities, we promote the following priority sub-competences in an accessible and affordable way: critical, systemic, innovative and scientific thinking. In doing so, we promote the development of creative and innovative solutions to real local and global problems and stimulate technology-based entrepreneurship in the scientific, technological and social fields.

SPECIFIC OBJECTIVES

1 First, we designed an online platform with features powered by Technologies 5.0 to foster scientific, technological and social entrepreneurship by training higher education students and lifelong learners in complex thinking.

2 Second, we experiment with, generate and transfer new knowledge through processes of design, creation and implementation in various educational contexts. We use mixed methods to obtain performance indices and assessment results that allow us to measure the impact on the development of complex thinking skills.

3 Finally, we create new products and services, generating the intellectual property of the Education 5.0 platform, including the technological platform, manuals, methodologies and teaching-learning programmes. We seek to promote the transfer of these resources to other higher education institutions, technology-based educational companies and entities with objectives aligned with those of our project.

Figure 2.
General and specific objectives of the OpenEdR4C platform

Objectives

Introduction

How can we promote the training of adults towards the development of skills for the entrepreneurship of the present and the construction of the future we want?

We know that our society faces increasingly urgent challenges, including climate change, access to quality education and decent employment to strengthen families and communities. The great problems that afflict the world and force us to make decisions and actions towards social transformation also place us in front of the need to educate ourselves in a different way. We are convinced that complex thinking is the path that allows us to tackle the challenges that the twenty-first century presents to us. Complex thinking is a mega competence that allows the interconnection of knowledge and experiences to visualise possibilities, innovate solutions and test them rigorously and systematically in a constantly changing society. The development of this competence is essential to being aware of the complexity of problems and the implications of their solutions (Morin & Pakman, 2003), as well as the resources available to reach them in innovative ways based on knowledge and technological development.

Although the panorama for developing entrepreneurship proposals around the world is very diverse, for those who wish to start a business in emerging countries, the challenges that are presented to them are based on the specificities of each region. According to Mageste et al. (2024), a determining factor in societies thriving in complex environments is the development of technical capacities or skills to implement profitable and economically sustainable projects over time. Fortunately, the conditions are in place for this. For example, the global growth is projected to keep 3.0 % in both 2023 and 2024, while the projected average growth is 1.6 % for South America, 2.7 % for Central America and Mexico and 2.8 % for the Caribbean (excluding Guyana) (ECLAC, 2024). The challenge now is to build greater, more dynamic and inclusive growth.

In this challenge, the OpenEdR4C project arises with the vision of offering a high-impact solution to solve problems in education and society through the effective and self-managed learning of entrepreneurship (Figure 3). The project promotes an open educational platform that contributes to the training of university students and adults in lifelong learning who wish to develop their complex thinking competence. In addition, through the improvement of skills concerning social, scientific and technological entrepreneurship and entrepreneurship projects connected to the particular contexts of each participant, the platform offers the possibility of providing solutions to the Sustainable Development Goals (SDGs) (UNESCO, 2016) while maintaining a global vision of the impact and relevance of each project.

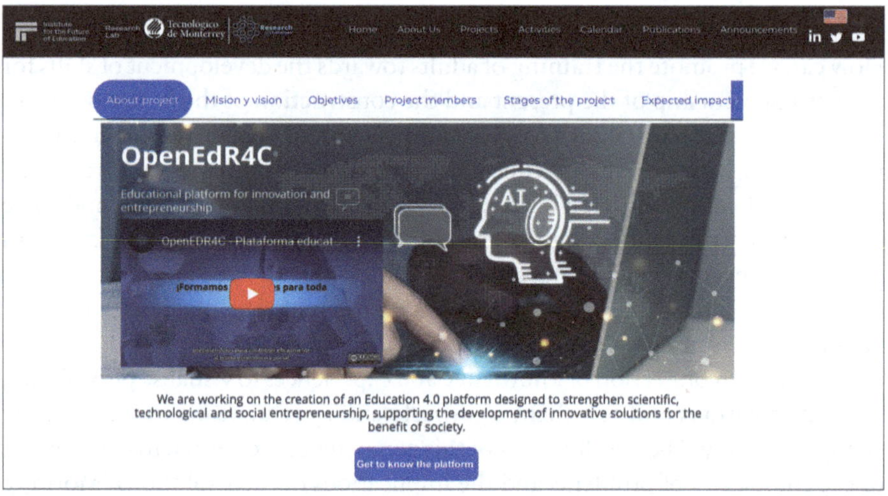

Figure 3. OpenEdR4C project website (https://www.research4challenges.world/en/openedr4c)

The OpenEDR4C (Figure 4) platform allows interested people to increase their knowledge and skills to create companies through the use of innovative ideas based on science, technology and social benefit and with environmental commitment. The educational content of this platform is designed to allow participants of varying profiles to find relevant resources that connect with their environment and to find the paths that lead to solutions in specific spaces. Taking diversity into account, a tool that gives attention to neurodiversity and sensory diversity has been included in the platform, adapting the characteristics of the interface to the preferences of each person.

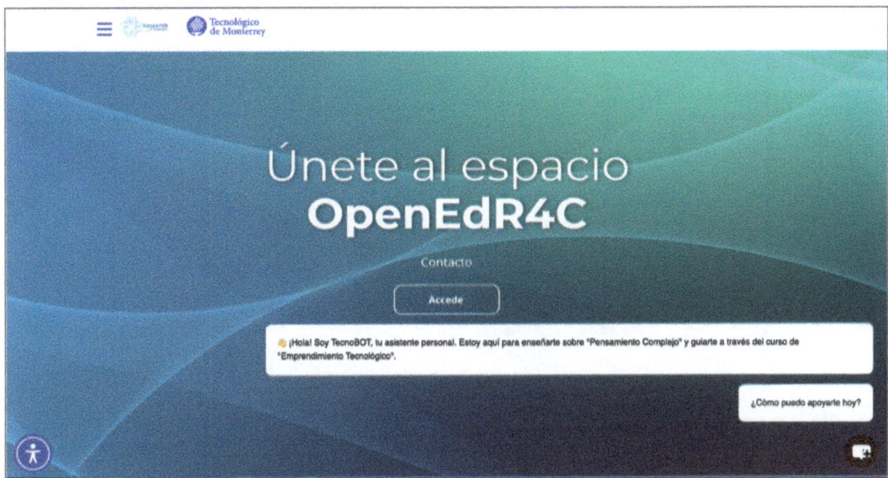

Figure 4. OpenEdR4C platform (https://openedr4c.world)

Finally, the resources, which are available for free download, cater to different learning styles and offer different means to reinforce knowledge and develop complex thinking sub-competencies. This open educational resource is a contribution to a new digital ecosystem in which everyone has quality resources at their fingertips to meet the challenges of a complex and constantly changing world. Let's direct that change towards the future we want so that it is fair, equitable, healthy and supportive.

References

Morin, E., & Pakman, M. (2003). Introduction to complex thinking (p. 167). Barcelona: gedisa.

Mageste, S., Plottier, C., Rocha, C., Saporito, N. (2024) Start-ups in Latin America and the Caribbean: A First Approach to Their Identification and Characteristics, Project Documents (LC/TS.2023/179), Santiago, Economic Commission for Latin America and the Caribbean (ECLAC). https://repositorio.cepal.org/server/api/core/bitstreams/278c3c03-ec4a-4cea-a33c-20c08a30b4ef/content

ECLAC (2024). Economies in Latin America and the Caribbean will grow 2.1 % in 2024, in a context of global uncertainty.https://www.cepal.org/es/comunicados/economias-america-latina-caribe-creceran-21-2024-un-contexto-incertidumbre-nivel-global

UNESCO (2016). Sustainable Development Goals. https://es.unesco.org/sdgs

How is Complex Thinking Linked to Entrepreneurship?

Complex thinking is a way of observing and interpreting reality that recognises and addresses the interconnectedness and multiplicity of factors present in various situations. Rather than simplifying reality ('what is observed') into smaller parts and analysing them one by one, complex thinking invites us to see situations in their entirety and consider how elements influence and relate to each other in ways that are often unexpected. This approach is particularly useful in times of great uncertainty or when we face problems that do not have easy answers, such as the phenomenon of climate change or economic crises. By adopting a complex thinking approach, we will be able to appreciate the diversity and dynamics that make up 'the total reality' in a general and objective way, allowing us to make more informed and effective decisions.

Social, scientific and technological entrepreneurship is deeply linked to the development of complex thinking, with competencies that encompass systemic, scientific, innovative and critical thinking. According to a study conducted by Vasquez-Parra et al. (2022), the validated eComplexity instrument (Castillo-Martínez & Ramírez-Montoya, 2022) was applied to 370 undergraduate students from various disciplines, showing that the areas of engineering, business and humanities excel in systems thinking, while architecture students excel in critical thinking. Another exploratory study by Ibarra-Vásquez et al. (2023) used the data from forty-seven students to analyse how complex thinking influences social entrepreneurship. The results indicate that, although previous family experiences do not directly influence the development of complex thinking competencies, they do help students become familiar with topics related to entrepreneurship. This shows that complex thinking is essential to facing global challenges and generating social value and contributes to innovation and sustainable progress in our society.

TO KNOW MORE …

On Complex Thinking and Its Link with Entrepreneurship

Let's change course: Lessons from the pandemic

Author: Edgar Morin
Reference: Morin, E. (2020). Let's change course: lessons from the pandemic. Paidós

▶ If you want to link complex thinking with entrepreneurship, we recommend Morin's work. Here, he highlights the importance of addressing reality while considering the interconnection and mutual influence of all its components, an especially relevant approach in times of crisis, such as the COVID-19 pandemic. This vision teaches us that, in order to generate innovative and sustainable solutions, we must integrate different dimensions of complex thinking into our initiatives. Applying complex thinking allows us to face global challenges with a holistic perspective, encouraging the creation of projects that not only address immediate problems but also contribute to long-term well-being.

Social entrepreneurship and complex thinking. Validation of methodology for the scaling of the perception of competence achievement

Authors: José Carlos Vázquez-Parra, J. C., Martina Carlos-Arroyo & Marco Cruz-Sandoval
Reference: Vázquez-Parra, J. C., Carlos-Arroyo, M. & Cruz-Sandoval, M. (2023). Social entrepreneurship and complex thinking. Validation of methodology for the scaling of the perception of competence achievement. Ed.Sc. 13(2). https://doi.org/10.3390/educsci13020186 Retrieved from: https://hdl.handle.net/11285/650172

▶ If you want to know more about complex thinking and entrepreneurship, we recommend reading about the Social Entrepreneurship Learning for Complexity (SEL4C) methodology developed by the Interdisciplinary Research Group Reasoning for Complexity at the Institute for the Future of Education at Tecnológico de Monterrey. This article presents a statistical analysis of an educational intervention carried out on students from a Mexican university, showing how this methodology not only improves social entrepreneurship competencies, but also develops complex thinking. The results validate that this methodology is effective in training essential transversal competences in the modern world. Together, we can learn to apply these tools to address global challenges and contribute to sustainable development.

Open model of complex thinking for the future of education

Authors: María Soledad Ramírez-Montoya, Fabián Eduardo Basabe, Martina Carlos Arroyo, Irma Azeneth Patiño Zúñiga, I. A. & May Portuguez Castro
Reference: Ramírez-Montoya, M. S., Basabe, E., Carlos Arroyo, M., Patiño Zúñiga, I. A., Portuguez Castro, M. (2024). Open model of complex thinking for the future of education. Octahedron. https://hdl.handle.net/11285/652033

▶ To discover more about complex thinking, we invite you to explore the innovative educational approach presented in this text. This approach is designed to respond to the demands of the modern world, integrating the following dimensions of thinking: critical, scientific, systemic and innovative. The objective is to train empathetic citizens committed to sustainable development. This model is not only applied in academic environments but also in government and business sectors, highlighting the importance of collaboration, empathy and commitment to sustainable solutions to global problems. By immersing yourself in this approach, you will be able to develop skills that will allow you to contribute meaningfully to society and the well-being of the planet.

The complex thinking competence is essential for the development of successful ventures, as it allows entrepreneurs to accept uncertainty and analyse the complex characteristics of the modern business world in depth. By approaching a business project with a complex thinking approach, entrepreneurs can better identify the interconnections between different areas of the market, anticipate potential challenges and opportunities, and adapt their strategies accordingly. This capacity for integrative analysis and adaptation is crucial to innovating and maintaining competitiveness in a dynamic and constantly evolving economic environment. Thus, complex thinking not only allows for improved decision-making and problem-solving but also boosts the ability of entrepreneurs to create more robust and sustainable business models.

References

Castillo-Martínez, I. M. & Ramírez-Montoya, M. S. (2022). Instrumento eComplexity: Medición de la percepción de estudiantes de educación superior acerca de su competencia de razonamiento para la complejidad. https://hdl.handle.net/11285/643622

Ibarra-Vazquez, G., Ramírez-Montoya, M. S., Miranda, J. (2023). Data Analysis in Factors of Social Entrepreneurship to Design Planning Tools in Complex Thinking. Thinking Skills and Creativity 40, 101381. https://doi.org/10.1016/j.tsc.2023.101381 https://hdl.handle.net/11285/651110

Vázquez-Parra, J. C.; Castillo-Martínez, I. M.; Ramírez-Montoya, M. S.; Millán, A. (2022). Development of the perception of achievement of complex thinking: A disciplinary approach in a Latin American student population. Education Sciences 12, Art. 289. https://doi.org/10.3390/educsci12050289 https://hdl.handle.net/11285/648187

Educational Innovation in Action

Innovation in open education allows free and open access to learning resources, breaking down economic and geographical barriers. The OpenEDR4C platform is an open educational resource, which means that its content can be accessed without needing to pay. It is designed to offer a self-managed and challenging training experience, facilitating progress in each of the topics and sections according to the pace of each participant. The content of each course was adapted according to the OEM4C (Ramírez-Montoya et al., 2024) using a very particular structure that combines approaches that foster the development of complex thinking competence and content that stimulates entrepreneurship to contribute to SDGs. In addition, different learning tools and strategies that allow a comprehensive and stimulating training experience are integrated into the platform.

As it is a self-managed platform, tools that enable asynchronous collaboration between participants are included, such as discussion forums where it is possible to learn about the concerns of other people from different contexts or countries who are working on the same topic. In the same way, participants were encouraged to use tools powered by artificial intelligence through a chatbot that offers information and teaches basic concepts about entrepreneurship and complex thinking. Additionally, strategies for visualising scenarios, defining relevant elements to consider and presenting videos have been integrated. All of these features allow participants to advance in the construction of entrepreneurship proposals with adequate skills and knowledge to turn their ideas into reality.

The platform allows interaction from different roles: student, administration and teacher. In the student role, courses are entered at the three levels of progress in each subject: basic, intermediate and advanced. Before starting each course, the platform asks participants to register and fill out a user profile. The platform uses this information to prepare reports on the progress of each participant. Once a participant completes the profile, they are asked to complete a diagnostic test before the platform grants them access to the courses.

With the teaching role, groups can be created, and reports on the performance of each student and the completion of courses, questionnaires and tests can be prepared. With this functionality, teachers can monitor the progress of their groups and know the needs of their students to suggest differentiated routes according to their learning pace. Groups are created, and each participant is assigned a course at an appropriate level (introductory, intermediate or advanced). Reports can be downloaded from the groups or for each course that has been selected, with a date range established in the creation of the groups.

The management role has specific attributes. An administrator can assign roles to each user, create groups, manage all groups and download general reports. The platform administrators in charge are members of the IRG-R4C Interdisciplinary Research Group Scaling Complex Thinking for All of the Institute for the Future of Education of Tecnológico de Monterrey. The monitoring from this role allows researchers in charge to use the information generated on the platform to develop knowledge about the best and most effective ways to develop complex thinking in the communities.

The 'Courses' page shows the areas assigned to each group, with each course having a welcome page that shows general details about the course, including an introduction, the objective, the approximate time to complete the course and the authorship of the content. The courses consist of four topics with four resources each. Quizzes and additional activities complement the educational experience, and the platform offers the freedom to move between content, allowing each participant to check, review, repeat and connect information. All resources on the platform are open educational resources (OER) and are protected by a Creative Common licence that allows them to be used outside the context of the platform. There are videos with subtitles that can be seen on the platform or on YouTube. There are also quizzes that provide instant feedback upon completion. Some activities are done without validation to be reflective, while others are collaborative and present the opportunity to interact with the ideas of other participants. You can also collaborate with other people through the discussion forum and with artificial intelligence (AI) agents through a chatbot. This robot is trained to provide answers related to the topic. It is not generative AI, although a generative tool is currently being designed to provide feedback on creative activities.

Reference

Ramírez-Montoya, M. S., Basabe, E., Carlos Arroyo, M., Patiño Zúñiga, I. A., Portuguez Castro, M. (2024). Modelo abierto de pensamiento complejo para el futuro de la educación. Octaedro. https://hdl.handle.net/11285/652033

WHAT DO THE STUDIES SAY …

About the Proposal Made from the Innovation Project?

Promoting scientific, social and technological entrepreneurship is essential to preparing students in higher education for the challenges of the present and the future. The platform is specially designed to help you develop your capabilities in these areas, an innovative digital context. This educational innovation tool not only teaches you the fundamentals of entrepreneurship but also helps you master complex thinking and its components: systemic, creative, innovative and scientific thinking. By using this platform, you can learn theoretical components while also applying these principles and theories to real projects that can have a significant impact on your community, taking into account the SDGs.

In this way, it is observed that scientific entrepreneurship allows you to transform discoveries and ideas from science into practical solutions that can improve your personal, family and social environment. With this platform, you could learn to identify scientific problems and develop innovative projects. In addition, the development of systemic thinking helps you understand how these problems connect with other aspects of society, how they are part of a whole and how they allow you to create complete, achievable and effective solutions (George-Reyes et al., 2023). By combining this with creative and scientific thinking, you'd be well-equipped to take your ideas from a classroom, a lab or an academic context into the real world.

Social and technological entrepreneurship is not only about creating new products using current technology or introducing new services to society; it is about generating a positive impact on society that is efficient, productive and immediate. This educational platform helps you think in an innovative way to develop projects that address important social problems using technology and makes you realise that you can do it. Complex thinking, which includes systemic, creative and innovative thinking, allows you to see the whole picture and find solutions that work efficiently and sustainably (Ramírez-Montoya et al., 2022). If you participate in this development, you can promote new forms of entrepreneurship and new ways of contributing to a world that is increasingly in need of adequate solutions, using your skills and knowledge to make a significant difference in your immediate environment.

References

George-Reyes, C., López-Caudana, E., & Lavonen, J. (2023). Complex and Design Thinking: Proof-of-Concept to Validate the i4C Methodology for Improving Scientific Entrepreneurship Skills. Onomázein (62),148–168. http://www.onomazein.com/index.php/onom/article/view/212 https://hdl.handle.net/11285/651470

Ramírez-Montoya, M. S., Castillo-Martínez, I. M., Sanabria-Zepeda, J. C., & Miranda, J. (2022). Complex Thinking in the Framework of Education 4.0 and Open Innovation—A Systematic Literature Review. Journal of Open Innovation: Technology, Market, and Complexity 8(4). https://doi.org/10.3390/joitmc8010004 https://repositorio.tec.mx/handle/11285/643380

WE INVITE YOU TO REFLECT …

How do you think social entrepreneurship can change the way we tackle the world's biggest problems, such as poverty, water scarcity or climate change?

Why do you think it is important to combine science and technology with entrepreneurship?

If you had the opportunity to create a startup with a scientific, social or technological base, what would be your main focus? What impact would you hope to achieve with your venture?

SDGs in Education

Within the framework of the SDGs, the OpenEDR4C platform contributes significantly to SDG 4, which seeks to ensure inclusive, equitable and quality education, promoting lifelong learning opportunities for all. By providing open educational resources and tools for complex skill development, OpenEDR4C facilitates access to high-quality education, especially in areas that have traditionally been underserved. This not only improves the quality of education but also democratises access to knowledge, giving students from diverse geographical spaces and socioeconomic contexts the opportunity to access the same learning opportunities.

Figure 5. SDGs mobilised through the OpenEdR4C platform

In addition to SDG 4, OpenEDR4C supports SDGs 5 and 10 (Figure 5), which focus on gender equality and reducing inequalities, respectively. The platform promotes an inclusive environment that encourages the participation of women and vulnerable groups in education and in the field of scientific entrepreneurship. By offering accessible resources and tools, OpenEDR4C helps close the gender gap in education and promotes equal opportunities, regardless of gender, ethnicity or socioeconomic status. In this way, the platform not only empowers women and other marginalised groups but also contributes to a more equitable and just society, aligned with the principles of the SDGs.

Reference

UNESCO (2016). Sustainable Development Goals. https://es.unesco.org/sdgs

TO KNOW MORE ...

The Link between the SDGs and the Proposal

Exploring entrepreneurship related to the sustainable development goals – mapping new venture activities with semi-automated content analysis

Authors: Jannic Horne, Malte Recker, Ingo Michelfelder, Jason Jay & Jan Kratzer

Reference: Horne, J., Recker, M., Michelfelder, I., Jay, J., & Kratzer, J. (2020). Exploring entrepreneurship related to the sustainable development goals - mapping new venture activities with semi-automated content analysis. Journal of Cleaner Production, 242, 118052. https://doi.org/10.1016/j.jclepro.2019.118052

▶ To find out more about the SDGs and entrepreneurship, we invite you to explore studies such as the study of Horne et al. (2020), which looks at how entrepreneurship in Germany contributes to SDGs. Using semi-automated content analysis, the authors of this study were able to map the activities of startups in relation to the SDGs, identifying patterns and areas of opportunity where entrepreneurship can have a significant impact on meeting these goals. By delving deeper into this type of research, you will not only learn how entrepreneurship can support sustainable development but also be able to identify ways in which you yourself can contribute to a more sustainable and equitable future.

Engagement and social impact in tech-based citizen Science initiatives for achieving the SDGs: a systematic literature review with a perspective on complex thinking

Authors: Jorge Sanabria-Z, Berenice Alfaro-Ponce, Omar Israel González Peña, Hugo Terashima-Marín & José Carlos Ortiz-Bayliss

Reference: Sanabria-Z, J.; Alfaro-Ponce, B.; González Peña, O. I.; Terashima-Marín, H.; & Ortiz-Bayliss, J. C. (2022). Engagement and Social Impact in Tech-Based Citizen Science Initiatives for Achieving the SDGs: A Systematic Literature Review with a Perspective on Complex Thinking. Sustainability 14(17), 10978. https://doi.org/10.3390/su141710978 https://repositorio.tec.mx/handle/11285/648805

▶ To learn more about complex thinking, the SDGs, and entrepreneurship, we recommend exploring advances in citizen science projects. These projects, which have made significant progress in recent years, address complex global challenges and support the 2030 SDG agenda. UNESCO highlights that citizen science can close gaps in science, technology and innovation, bringing ordinary people closer to these fields. A recent study reviewed forty-nine citizen science projects and found that, although these projects are widely implemented in Europe and focus on issues such as the built environment and environmental monitoring, there is still a huge opportunity to develop native technologies and increase citizen participation. This not only achieves a greater social impact but also encourages the development of complex thinking skills in participants. We invite you to join these initiatives, which benefit the community and can help you improve your ability to analyse and solve complex problems.

New Educational Scenarios

EDUCATIONAL SCENARIO aimed at students

Learn about scientific entrepreneurship on the OpenEDR4C platform: Scientific entrepreneurship ecosystem

Linked SDGs

Activity

In this activity, you will explore the concept of scientific entrepreneurship using the OpenEDR4C platform. You will learn how scientific knowledge can contribute to the transformation of companies by making them innovative, contributing to technological development and favouring the resolution of local and global problems. Throughout this experience, you will discover OpenEDR4C's digital ecosystem, which fosters the understanding of scientific entrepreneurship.

Objective

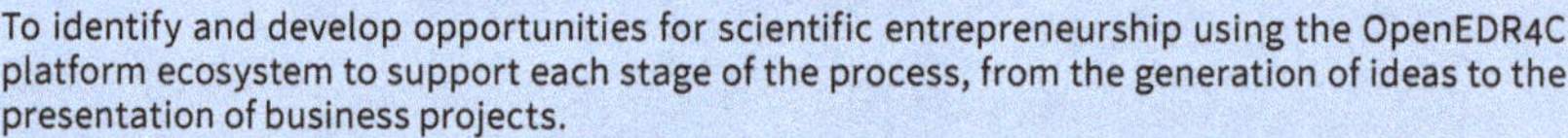

To identify and develop opportunities for scientific entrepreneurship using the OpenEDR4C platform ecosystem to support each stage of the process, from the generation of ideas to the presentation of business projects.

Beginning

1. Register for OpenEDR4C and take the initial diagnostic assessment to learn about your skills in complex thinking and entrepreneurship.
2. Watch the welcome video, which explains the course objectives and how to navigate the platform to get the most out of the interactive content and tools.

Development

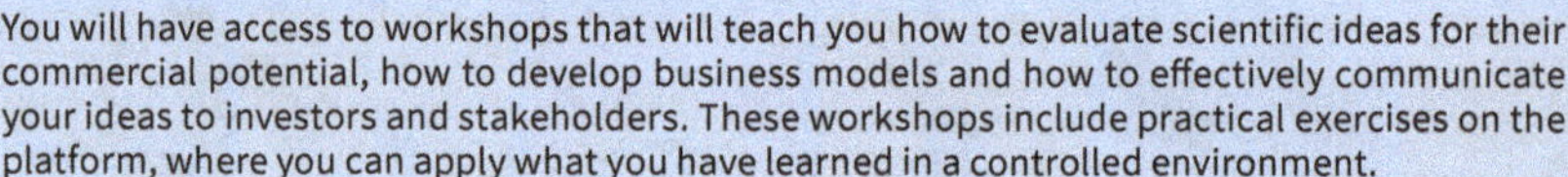

You will have access to workshops that will teach you how to evaluate scientific ideas for their commercial potential, how to develop business models and how to effectively communicate your ideas to investors and stakeholders. These workshops include practical exercises on the platform, where you can apply what you have learned in a controlled environment.

Using OpenEDR4C's online development tools, you will work on crafting your business idea. The platform facilitates real-time interaction and project management, allowing you to share documents, give and receive feedback and update your progress.

Throughout the course, you will complete formative assessments that will help you understand your progress and areas for improvement. These assessments are integrated into the platform and are essential to ensuring that you achieve the established learning objectives.

Closing

At the end of the course, you will submit a project that will be evaluated using a scientific entrepreneurship rubric. You will receive detailed feedback that you can use to improve your proposals or prepare for future entrepreneurship opportunities.

Participants who satisfactorily complete all parts of the course will receive a digital certificate through the platform that acknowledges their participation and achievement of the objectives.

Evaluation

The evaluation process will be carried out in a variety of ways:

- Formative evaluations: During the development of the activity, periodic evaluations will be carried out on the platform along with self-evaluations. These assessments will allow you to receive immediate feedback on your progress and better understand the key concepts of scientific entrepreneurship.
- Questionnaires to assess the development of competencies: Perception questionnaires will be used to measure the development of competencies in complex thinking and entrepreneurship.
- Scientific entrepreneurship rubric: The rubric considers four dimensions of analysis: collaboration, knowledge, project design and research skills. It assesses the entrepreneurial skills developed by the students.

Evidence of Learning

To evidence your participation, activity records will be taken from the OpenEDR4C platform, including answers to knowledge and perception questionnaires and the activities that you must complete and submit on the platform.

Digital Materials or Tools

To effectively perform the activity on the OpenEDR4C platform, you will need the following:

- Access to OpenEDR4C: Easily achieved using an email account.
- Mobile Devices: You can use smartphones, tablets, laptops, or desktops.
- Internet access: Essential to participating in all activities and using the platform's tools.

EDUCATIONAL SCENARIO aimed at teachers

Educational scenario for teachers in the OpenEDR4C platform: Scientific entrepreneurship

Linked SDGs

Activity

This activity is designed for teachers who will explore the OpenEDR4C platform and the scientific entrepreneurship course. In this experience, you will learn how scientific knowledge can contribute to the transformation of companies by making them innovative, contributing to technological development and favouring the resolution of local and global problems. You will get to know the OpenEDR4C digital ecosystem, which will help you understand what scientific entrepreneurship is and how you can guide students in this area of knowledge.

Objective

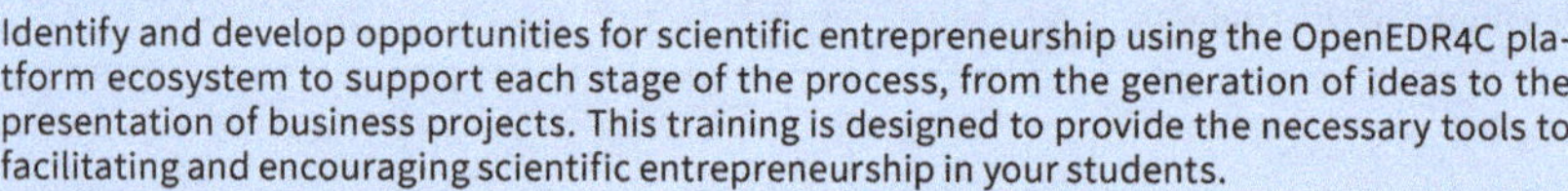

Identify and develop opportunities for scientific entrepreneurship using the OpenEDR4C platform ecosystem to support each stage of the process, from the generation of ideas to the presentation of business projects. This training is designed to provide the necessary tools to facilitating and encouraging scientific entrepreneurship in your students.

Beginning

1. Sign up for OpenEDR4C and complete the initial diagnostic assessment to measure your competencies in complex thinking and entrepreneurship.
2. Watch the welcome video, which explains in detail the objectives of the course and how you can use the platform to maximise the benefits of the content and interactive tools available.

Development

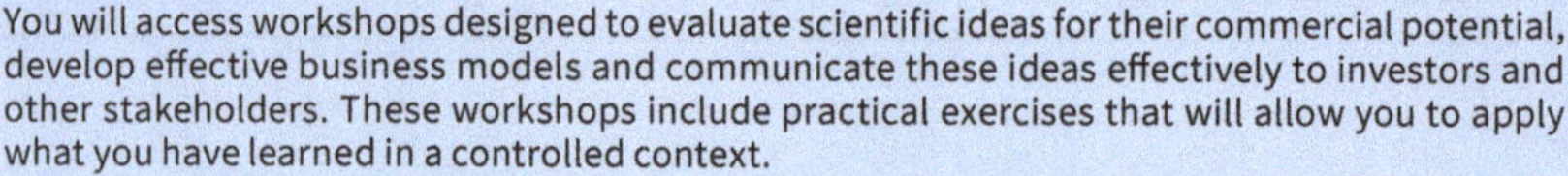

You will access workshops designed to evaluate scientific ideas for their commercial potential, develop effective business models and communicate these ideas effectively to investors and other stakeholders. These workshops include practical exercises that will allow you to apply what you have learned in a controlled context.

Using OpenEDR4C's tools, you will work on developing your own business ideas. The platform facilitates real-time interaction and project management, allowing you to share documents, receive and offer feedback and monitor your progress.

Throughout the course, you'll conduct formative assessments built into the platform, helping you understand your progress and areas for improvement. These assessments are crucial to ensuring that you achieve learning objectives.

Closing

At the end of the course, you will present your scientific entrepreneurship project, which will be evaluated using a rubric designed to measure the feasibility, innovation and impact potential of the project. You will receive detailed feedback, which is essential to improving your proposals and preparing you to lead future entrepreneurship initiatives.

Teachers who satisfactorily complete all stages of the course will receive a digital certificate through the platform in recognition of their participation and achievement of the objectives. This certificate will serve as recognition of your ability to guide and motivate your students in scientific entrepreneurship projects.

Evaluation

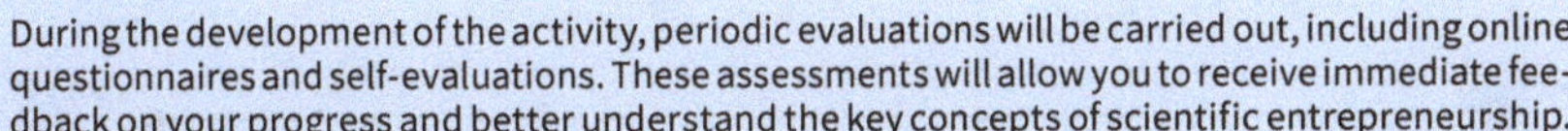

During the development of the activity, periodic evaluations will be carried out, including online questionnaires and self-evaluations. These assessments will allow you to receive immediate feedback on your progress and better understand the key concepts of scientific entrepreneurship.

Perception questionnaires will be used to measure the development of competencies in complex thinking and entrepreneurship.

Evidence of Learning

To evidence your participation, activity records will be taken from the OpenEDR4C platform, including answers to knowledge and perception questionnaires and the activities that you must upload to the platform.

Digital Materials or Tools

- Access to OpenEDR4C: Easily achieved using an email account.
- Mobile Devices: You can use smartphones, tablets, laptops or desktops.
- Internet access: Essential to participating in all activities and using the platform's tools.

EDUCATIONAL SCENARIO aimed at companies

Scientific entrepreneurship activity on the OpenEDR4C platform: Oriented to companies

Linked SDGs

Activity

OpenEDR4C allows companies to explore and expand their horizons in the world of scientific entrepreneurship. This activity is focused on the transformation of scientific knowledge into commercial innovations that not only drive business growth but also contribute to solving local and global problems.

Objective

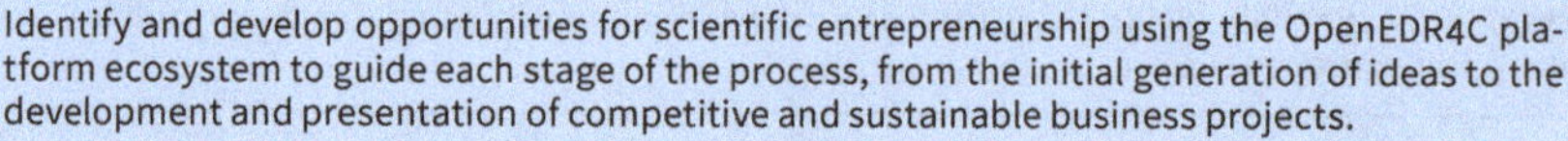

Identify and develop opportunities for scientific entrepreneurship using the OpenEDR4C platform ecosystem to guide each stage of the process, from the initial generation of ideas to the development and presentation of competitive and sustainable business projects.

Beginning

- Sign up for OpenEDR4C and complete the initial diagnostic assessment to map your current competencies in complex thinking and entrepreneurship.
- Watch the welcome video, which explains in detail the objectives of the course and provides guidance on how to navigate the platform, helping you maximise the use of the content and interactive tools.

Development

You will have access to expert-led workshops, through which you will increase skills to evaluate the commercial potential of scientific ideas, develop robust business models and effectively communicate your ideas to investors and other relevant stakeholders. These workshops include practical exercises on the platform, facilitating the direct application of the knowledge acquired.

You will use OpenEDR4C's tools to work on formulating and refining your own business ideas. The platform offers resources to facilitate real-time interaction, project management, document sharing, receiving and giving feedback and monitoring progress continuously.

You'll complete formative assessments designed to help you assess your progress and identify areas for improvement. These assessments are integrated into the platform and are crucial to ensuring that you achieve the learning objectives set.

Closing

At the end of the workshop, you will present your scientific entrepreneurship project, which will be evaluated according to a specialised rubric in scientific entrepreneurship. These presentations will provide you with an opportunity to receive detailed feedback, which you can use to refine your pitches or prepare for future opportunities.

Participants who satisfactorily complete all stages of the course will receive a digital certificate through the platform in recognition of their active participation and the fulfilment of the objectives. This certificate can serve as a differentiator in the market, highlighting your commitment to innovation and continuous development.

Evaluation

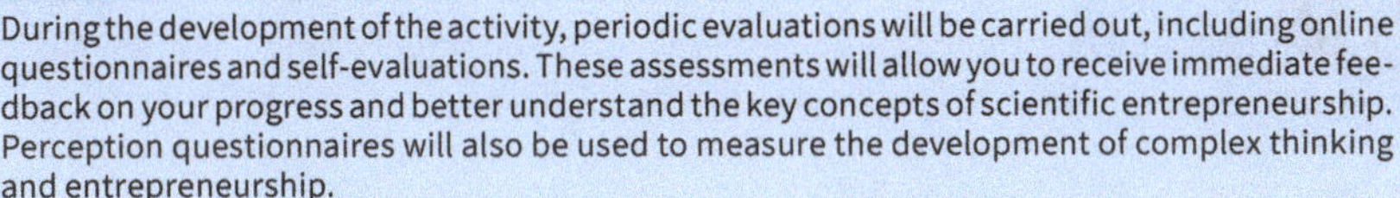

During the development of the activity, periodic evaluations will be carried out, including online questionnaires and self-evaluations. These assessments will allow you to receive immediate feedback on your progress and better understand the key concepts of scientific entrepreneurship. Perception questionnaires will also be used to measure the development of complex thinking and entrepreneurship.

Evidence of Learning

To evidence your participation, activity records will be taken from the OpenEDR4C platform, including answers to the knowledge and perception questionnaires and the activities requested by the platform.

Digital Materials or Tools

- Access to OpenEDR4C: Easily achieved using an email account.
- Mobile Devices: You can use smartphones, tablets, laptops, or desktops.
- Internet access: Essential to participating in all activities and using the platform's tools.

EDUCATIONAL SCENARIO aimed at NGOs

Scientific entrepreneurship activity in the OpenEDR4C platform for NGOs

Linked SDGs

Activity

This experience is aimed at showing how scientific knowledge can be transformed into innovative initiatives that not only contribute to technological development but also address local and global challenges. During this activity, you will explore the OpenEDR4C platform and discover how your organisation can generate positive change by responding to current social issues.

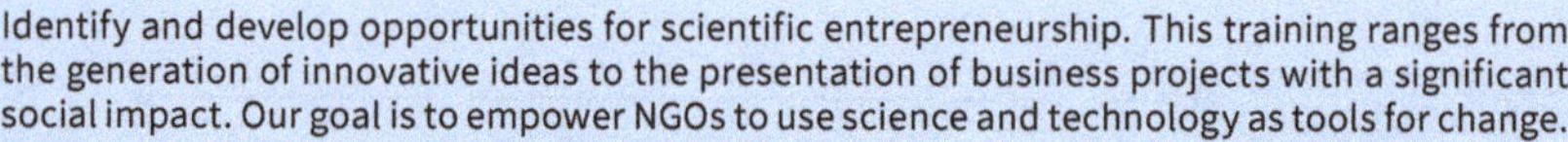

Objective

Identify and develop opportunities for scientific entrepreneurship. This training ranges from the generation of innovative ideas to the presentation of business projects with a significant social impact. Our goal is to empower NGOs to use science and technology as tools for change.

Beginning

- Sign up for OpenEDR4C and take a diagnostic assessment to measure your skills in complex thinking and entrepreneurship. This is crucial to tailoring the course to your specific needs.
- Check out the welcome video, which explains the course objectives in detail and guides you on how to navigate the platform to get the most out of the educational content and interactive tools.

Development

You will have access to workshops where you will learn how to evaluate scientific ideas for their commercial and social potential, how to develop sustainable business models, and how to effectively communicate your ideas to investors and key stakeholders. These workshops include practical exercises on the platform, allowing you to apply what you have learned in a controlled and collaborative environment.

You will use OpenEDR4C's online development tools to craft your business ideas. The platform facilitates real-time interaction and project management, allowing NGOs to share documents, receive and give feedback and update their progress.

You'll complete formative assessments throughout the course to monitor your progress and identify areas for improvement. These assessments, which are integrated into the platform, are essential to ensuring that you achieve the proposed learning objectives.

Closing

At the end of the activity, you will present your scientific entrepreneurship project, which will be evaluated through a rubric focused on social impact and feasibility. Participants who satisfactorily complete all parts of the course will receive a digital certificate through the platform, acknowledging their participation and success in achieving the learning objectives.

Evaluation

During the development of the activity, periodic evaluations will be carried out, including online questionnaires and self-evaluations. These assessments will allow you to receive immediate feedback on your progress and better understand the key concepts of scientific entrepreneurship. Perception questionnaires will be used to measure the development of complex thinking and entrepreneurship.

Evidence of Learning

To evidence the implementation, user activity records taken from the OpenEDR4C platform, including responses to knowledge and perception questionnaires and the activities requested by the platform will be taken.

Digital Materials or Tools

- Access to OpenEDR4C, which is very easily achieved using an email account.
- Mobile devices such as smartphones or tablets, laptops and desktop computers can be used.
- Internet access.

EDUCATIONAL SCENARIO aimed at lifelong learning

Introduction to the scientific entrepreneurship activity at OpenEDR4C

Linked SDGs

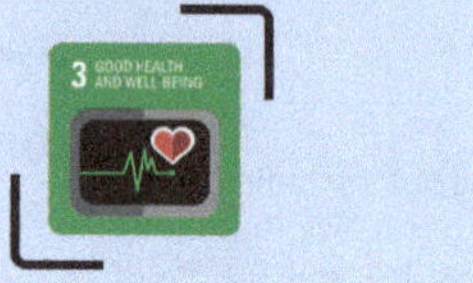

Activity

Welcome to this educational experience of the OpenEDR4C platform, designed especially for people who are committed to continuous lifelong learning. Here, you'll explore how scientific entrepreneurship can transform knowledge into innovative companies that not only lead the market but also tackle some of the most challenging global problems. Throughout this activity, you will discover the dynamic ecosystem of scientific entrepreneurship and learn how to actively integrate yourself into this field, no matter what stage of your professional career you are in.

Objective

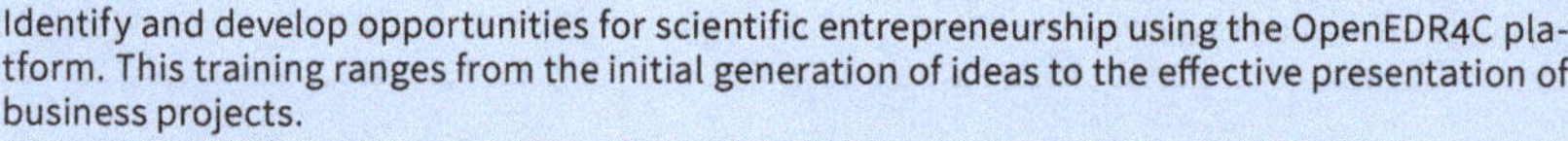

Identify and develop opportunities for scientific entrepreneurship using the OpenEDR4C platform. This training ranges from the initial generation of ideas to the effective presentation of business projects.

Beginning

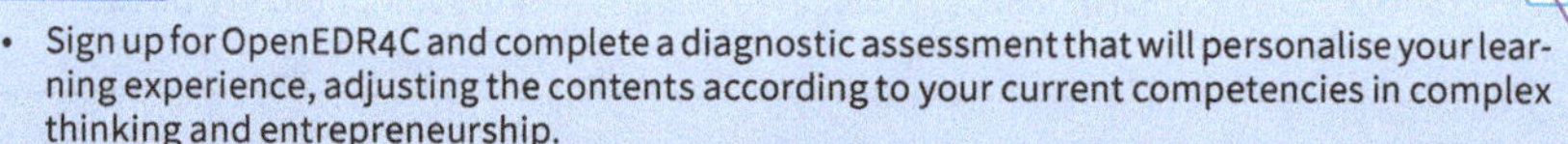

- Sign up for OpenEDR4C and complete a diagnostic assessment that will personalise your learning experience, adjusting the contents according to your current competencies in complex thinking and entrepreneurship.
- Check out the explanatory video, which shows you how to navigate the platform. This will help you maximise the use of available content and interactive tools, ensuring that you can easily access everything you need to succeed in the course.

Development

You'll participate in workshops designed to teach you how to evaluate the commercial potential of scientific ideas, develop sound business models and effectively communicate your ideas to potential investors and other stakeholders.

You will use OpenEDR4C's online development tools to craft your business ideas. The platform facilitates real-time interaction and project management, allowing you to share documents, receive and give feedback and keep track of your progress.

Complete the platform's built-in assessments throughout the course to measure your progress and identify areas for improvement. These assessments are essential to ensuring that you achieve the established learning objectives.

Closing

As a final activity, you will present your scientific entrepreneurship project, which will be evaluated using a detailed rubric. Participants who satisfactorily complete all parts of the course will receive a digital certificate through the platform, acknowledging their active participation and achievement of the objectives.

Evaluation

During the development of the activity, periodic evaluations will be carried out, including online questionnaires and self-evaluations. These assessments will allow you to receive immediate feedback on your progress and better understand the key concepts of scientific entrepreneurship. Perception questionnaires will be used to measure the scaling of complex thinking and entrepreneurship.

Evidence of Learning

To evidence the activity, user records will be taken from the OpenEDR4C platform, including responses to knowledge and perception questionnaires and the activities requested on the platform.

Digital Materials or Tools

- Access to OpenEDR4C: easily achieved using an email account.
- Mobile devices: smartphones or tablets as well as laptops and desktop computers.
- Internet access: essential to participating in all activities and using the platform's tools.

Define our goals in the medium and long term, recognising our capacities and needs. Understanding what value the platform has for our community will depend on defining how it can help us meet our individual or collective goals. The role we play in the present may be the starting point, but it is important to imagine where we want to go (define the goals) and how the capabilities that can be developed on the platform can contribute to achieve the goals set before.

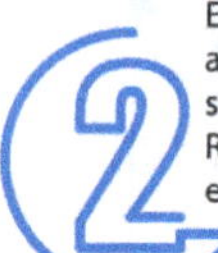

Establish a framework of reference with the Sustainable Development Goals. Each participant will have a different priority. For example, each student would want to start a business as soon as they finish their studies, while faculty members would want to have updated and valuable tools for their courses. Recognising the problems of our community that we want to solve through the development of entrepreneurial ideas will help us direct our efforts.

Set the scope of the entrepreneurship proposals that will be generated in the course. This definition will allow us to make proposals with a greater level of detail, and the solutions will allow us to generate a change in our societies. In the case of adults in training, for example, defining whether they will arrive at a minimum viable product or a presentation to obtain investment establishes two complementary—but different—routes of action.

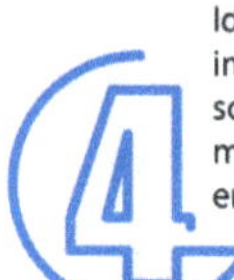

Identify who we want to benefit from our proposal, imagining the future we want. At this stage it is very important to ask ourselves how to include different groups of people who need to benefit from this solution as well as the different roles involved, including partners, licensees, clients and investors. We must also consider the people from different sectors of society who can benefit from our entrepreneurship proposal.

Construct an entrepreneurship proposal based on the knowledge acquired in the previous stages. The intention is to promote the search for innovative solutions and the generation of proposals that benefit the selected community in a creative and sustainable way through scientific, technological or social entrepreneurship.

Evaluate the training experience. The last phase of the implementation will focus on evaluating the capacities developed during the training experience. Participants will be able to make a reflective self-evaluation to determine how much the experience contributed to them. However, for the group of teachers and trainers, they will also be able to make use of the reports to review the progress of their groups in training and take actions to reinforce the competence development with practice or continue on a successful path.

Figure 6.
Recommendations for implementing the OpenEdR4C platform

Recommendations for Implementation

The implementation of the OpenEDR4C platform will be different for each of the contexts in which it is adopted and the roles of the participants – whether they are students, teachers, companies, adults in training throughout their lives and those who work towards the achievement of the SDGs from various fronts of action. For each sector, the implementation recommendations will have different approaches; however, all of them focus on the construction of a training scenario in which the development of the four sub-competencies of complex thinking – scientific, critical, systemic and innovative thinking – is considered. But how can we include these elements in scenarios that can be visualised from different approaches and that promote solutions to global challenges based on entrepreneurship?

The following list will help you establish a suitable guideline for the implementation of the OpenEdR4C platform in each of the relevant sectors (Figure 6).

Case Study: Entrepreneurship to Address Access to Drinking Water in Rural Communities

In a rural community, the lack of access to drinking water is a problem that affects the health and quality of life of its inhabitants. Many have to walk long distances to obtain water from unsafe sources, which increases the incidence of diseases and limits the time available for productive activities. In response, a group of entrepreneurs decides to develop a project that combines technology, science, and social entrepreneurship to improve access to drinking water.

The entrepreneurial team uses scientific knowledge to develop an affordable water purification system that can be adapted to rural conditions. This system uses solar energy to operate independently, without the need for an electrical grid. Additionally, its modular design allows it to be adapted to different water volumes, which is crucial in communities of varying sizes.

To implement the project, the group launches a crowdfunding campaign, raising awareness among individuals and institutions about the importance of supporting sustainable solutions for water access. The goal is to install this system in strategic places within the community and train its inhabitants in its use and maintenance, thereby promoting self-management and sustainability of the project. Additionally, they explore partnerships with NGOs to expand the project's reach to other communities in similar situations.

How Does the OpenEDR4C Platform Work to Solve the Case?

The OpenEDR4C platform follows a structured approach to address the case. Here's an explanation of the process:

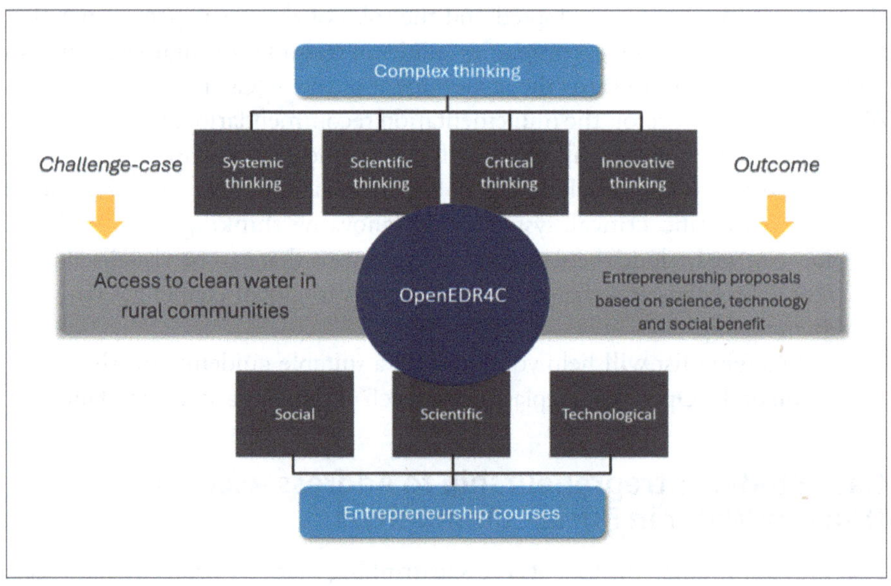

1. Challenge-Case: The first step involves presenting a real problem or challenge – in this case, access to drinking water in rural communities.
2. Complex Thinking: The platform fosters different sub-competencies of complex thinking, which are key to tackling complex problems:
   a. Systemic Thinking: Allows for analysing the case from a holistic perspective, understanding the interconnections between the various factors influencing access to drinking water.

   b. Scientific Thinking: Utilises an evidence-based approach to investigate causes and potential scientific solutions.
   c. Critical Thinking: Promotes critical evaluation of the information and proposed solutions.
   d. Innovative Thinking: Encourages the generation of novel ideas to solve the problem creatively.
3. OpenEDR4C as a Hub: The platform integrates these types of thinking, serving as a central hub where users (students or entrepreneurs) can work on solutions to the presented challenge.
4. Entrepreneurship Courses: OpenEDR4C includes entrepreneurship courses in three fundamental areas:
   a. Social: To address the social impact of the proposals.
   b. Scientific: Focused on solutions grounded in scientific knowledge.
   c. Technological: Oriented toward the creation of technological solutions for the problem.
5. Output – Entrepreneurship Proposals: Finally, the goal is to generate entrepreneurship proposals that benefit the community, using approaches based on science, technology, and social benefits. These proposals represent a concrete and applicable outcome of the work conducted on the platform.

Reflection questions

Scientific Entrepreneurship

Which of the following is an appropriate strategy to validate the effectiveness of the water purification system developed in this case?

a) Conduct laboratory and field tests to evaluate their efficiency and adaptability. ☑
b) Use only mathematical models to estimate their effectiveness in the field.
c) Test the system only in laboratory conditions without considering environmental variables.

Social Entrepreneurship

What is a fundamental aspect of social entrepreneurship according to the approach in this case?

a) Create a product that is exclusive to a minority who can afford it.
b) Develop solutions that benefit the community and contribute to social well-being. ☑
c) Focus solely on maximising the company's economic profits.

Technological Entrepreneurship

What is the appropriate approach to implementing technology in a rural context like the one described?

a) Use advanced technology without considering local needs and capabilities.
b) Develop a technology that requires no maintenance and can operate without supervision.
c) Implement accessible, easy-to-maintain technology adapted to the availability of local resources. ☑

OPEN EDUCATIONAL RESOURCES (OER)

OER: Educational entrepreneurship – UNESCO chair open educational movement for LATAM 2023
Authors: María Soledad Ramírez Montoya, M. S., & Jhonattan Miranda Mendoza
Reference: Ramírez Montoya, M. S., & Miranda Mendoza, J. (2024). Educational entrepreneurship—UNESCO chair open educational movement for LATAM 2023 [Video]. https://hdl.handle.net/11285/676164

▶ We invite you to immerse yourself in an inspiring educational resource in video format. This material focuses on the fascinating world of educational entrepreneurship and highlights the incredible experiences and projects of several participants in the UNESCO Chair Open Educational Movement residency for Latin America. Imagine that we are exploring how these projects are transforming education, bringing innovations and solutions that truly make a difference. This video will not only allow you to learn about these inspiring stories but also motivate you to see how you yourself can contribute to educational development. Join this learning community, and let's discover the positive impact we can make together. Let's learn by building!

OER: TecnoEmprendimiento – Technology-based solutions for the sustainable development goals
Author: Jhonattan Miranda Mendoza
Reference: Miranda Mendoza, J. (2024). TecnoEmprendimiento - Technology-based solutions for the sustainable development goals [Video]. https://hdl.handle.net/11285/676169

▶ We share an exciting educational video resource that you can't miss. This video features a fascinating workshop focused on technological entrepreneurship and the implementation of Education 4.0. Together, we will discover how new technologies can be integrated into education to enhance learning and foster innovation. Through practical examples and enriching discussions, this workshop offers us valuable strategies for all those who wish to undertake practice in the education sector. Imagine that we are in this workshop, learning and collaborating, sharing ideas and solutions. Join this learning community, and, together, let's discover how we can transform education with technology. Let's innovate together!

OER: Building diverse, open environments for all: The education of the future
Authors: Inés Alvarez-Icaza & Adolfo Rodríguez
Reference: Alvarez-Icaza, I. & Rodríguez, A. (2024). Building diverse, open environments for all: The education of the future [Video]. Webcast program: Future of education in complexity. Tecnológico de Monterrey. https://hdl.handle.net/11285/676177

▶ We invite you to explore an educational video resource that will make you feel part of a community dedicated to the education of the future. Imagine that we are together, building diverse, open and accessible environments for all. This video aims to showcase and compile strategies that will help us create inclusive and accessible educational resources for all. Through this shared experience, we will learn how to design materials that reach more people and foster more equitable education. Join this adventure, and let's discover how we can contribute to a more inclusive educational future together. Let's learn as a community!

OER: Exploring the potential of AI in competency assessment
Authors: Jorge Carlos Sanabria Zepeda & Pamela Geraldine Olivo Montaño
Reference: Sanabria Zepeda, J. C. & Olivo Montaño, P. G. (2024). Exploring the Potential of AI in Competency Assessment [Video]. Webcast program: Future of education in complexity. Tecnológico de Monterrey. https://hdl.handle.net/11285/651643

▶ We share an educational video resource that promises to open new doors in the field of education. Imagine that we are facing this great challenge together: measuring complex thinking and discovering how artificial intelligence (AI) can automate this process. This topic may seem controversial because AI would replace the role traditionally played by an instructor in assessment. In this video, we present you with a fascinating case study on an AI-powered platform used in the CxT Ideathon, along with the first results of this innovative application from the OpenEd4C Challenge project. Join me on this educational adventure to understand how technology can transform our teaching and assessment methodologies. Let's evolve together!

OER: Adaptive evaluation for barriers elimination: The OpenEDR4C platform
Authors: Inés Álvarez Icaza Longoria, José Martín Molina Espinosa, Paloma Suárez Brito & Ignacio Alvarado Reyes
Reference: Álvarez-Icaza, I., Suárez-Brito, P. & Molina-Espinosa, J. M., (2024) Adaptive Evaluation for Barriers Elimination: The OpenEDR4C Platform [Text]. 12th International Conference on Information and Education Technology (ICIET 2024) https://doi.org/10.1109/ICIET60671.2024.10542786 https://hdl.handle.net/11285/653803

▶ This fascinating educational resource, presented at an international conference, addresses a crucial challenge in our times: bridging the digital and educational divide between marginalised students and lifelong learners in the context of Industry and Education 4.0 paradigms. This text explains how adaptive learning has become a key strategy to increase student engagement, promoting inclusion, equity and better educational outcomes. The study presents us with three valuable contributions: a tool for conceptualising inclusive and accessible platforms, a framework for adaptive learning profiles and the identification of classes of users based on their needs and characteristics. Join me on this learning experience, and let's discover how this platform can transform digital education and make it accessible to everyone together. Let's grow in community!

CALL TO ACTION

Your voice and your ideas are crucial to building a better future together!
The global challenges we face require collaboration and harnessing a diversity of thought and skills. That's why we invite you to join us in this mission. Whether you have innovative projects, ongoing research, ideas you want to put into practice or a desire to empower your community, we want to work with you. From civil society, schools and universities to businesses and legislative groups, each sector has a unique perspective that can enrich our approach. Help us drive complex thinking and social, scientific and technological entrepreneurship.

Let's create a future full of opportunities and sustainable solutions together!
Our research group: https://tec.mx/es/r4c-irg
Explore our projects: https://www.research4challenges.world/

Join the project OpenEdR4C platform:
https://www.research4challenges.world/openedr4c

GLOSSARY

Complex thinking: Complex thinking is the competence of observing reality by considering the totality of the factors that converge to shape it. Rather than focusing on each factor in isolation, it is understood that each part contributes to and is influenced by the totality of reality. This integrative approach allows us to understand how the different parts are interrelated and affect each other, providing a more complete and in-depth view of the world.

Education 5.0: A form of education that relies on technology to facilitate personalised experiences, enriched with didactic resources and active strategies to facilitate learning and attention to diversity. It is linked to the demands of the labour market in digital capabilities, automation and artificial intelligence to enhance productivity and human well-being.

Scientific entrepreneurship: Action that contains the application of scientific knowledge and discoveries for the creation of new companies or innovative and disruptive products that solve challenges and/or the needs of a community or company. This action involves the identification of business opportunities based on scientific research and technological development.

Social entrepreneurship: It focuses on creating, evaluating and pursuing opportunities that positively transform communities and productive systems and increase economic value. This type of entrepreneurship values environmental and social sustainability and focuses on supporting changemakers who are committed to the mission of the social enterprise. Simply put, these are businesses that not only make money but also make positive and lasting impacts on society.

Sustainable Development Goals (SDGs): The SDGs are a set of global and concrete action-oriented goals whose purpose is to protect the planet, eradicate poverty and achieve peace and prosperity for all people. Each SDG includes several specific targets that detail how to achieve each goal, promoting a comprehensive approach to sustainable development around the world.

Technological entrepreneurship: The process of creating, developing and managing companies or projects that use technology in an innovative way to offer disruptive products or services in the market. In addition, tech entrepreneurship involves identifying technology-intensive business opportunities, pooling resources and managing significant growth and risk. This definition underlines how technological entrepreneurship differs from other types of entrepreneurships, focusing on technology as the core of a new enterprise or on the substantial incorporation of new technologies into the operation or design of a project.

Contenido

ESPAÑOL

Educación 5.0 para Movilizar Emprendimiento Social, Científico y Tecnológico

Plataforma OpenEdR4C

María Soledad Ramírez-Montoya

(Doctora en Filosofía y Ciencias de la Educación)

Inés Alvarez Icaza Longoria

(Doctora en Ingeniería)

Edgar Omar López Caudana

(Doctor en Comunicaciones y Electrónica)

Carlos Enrique George Reyes

(Doctor en Ciencias de la Educación)

Paloma Suárez Brito

(Doctora en Psicología)

Pamela Geraldine Olivo Montaño

(Doctora en Filosofía de la Ciencia)

Figura 1.
Investigadores del R4C-IRG movilizadores de la Plataforma OpenEdR4C

Sobre Nosotros

Somos integrantes del grupo de investigación R4C-IRG: Escalando el pensamiento complejo para todos (Figura 1), nos apasiona llevar la educación superior a nuevos niveles de excelencia. Nos dedicamos a desarrollar y promover competencias avanzadas de razonamiento para enfrentar la complejidad del mundo moderno. Utilizamos estrategias de Ciencia Abierta y las más avanzadas Tecnologías 5.0 como la inteligencia artificial y la ciencia de datos, para crear sistemas formativos que preparen a las personas para los desafíos del futuro. Nuestra labor se enlaza con proyectos que integran la universidad, la industria, el gobierno y el sector civil, buscando siempre soluciones sostenibles que beneficien a toda la sociedad.

Nuestra visión es clara y ambiciosa: contribuir de manera significativa al futuro de la educación, creando soluciones innovadoras para los problemas y retos de la sociedad actual. Nos alineamos con los objetivos de la agenda 2030 de la UNESCO para el desarrollo sostenible, fomentando la colaboración interdisciplinaria y la construcción de redes académicas robustas. En R4C-IRG, trabajamos para formar una nueva generación de profesionales altamente competitivos y comprometidos con el bienestar social, siempre buscando habilitar soluciones innovadoras que respondan a los retos presentes y futuros.

Carta Editorial

Empezamos un emocionante proyecto para desarrollar, experimentar e implementar una plataforma educativa en línea OpenEDR4C caracterizada por funciones y servicios basados en inteligencia artificial, interfaces multimedia interactivas y gamificadas, impulsadas por Tecnologías 5.0. Esta plataforma, basada en la Educación 5.0, busca fomentar el emprendimiento científico, tecnológico y social a través de la formación en competencias de pensamiento complejo para estudiantes de educación superior y personas en aprendizaje continuo sin olvidar el factor humano.

Nuestro objetivo en el proyecto OpenEdR4C: Plataforma de Educación 5.0 para fortalecer el Emprendimiento Científico, Tecnológico y Social a través de escalar Competencias de Pensamiento Complejo es invitar a las personas beneficiarias a participar en dinámicas de aprendizaje activas en entornos complejos del mundo real, promoviendo así la creación de soluciones tecnológicas para problemas prioritarios en contextos específicos. La plataforma tiene como sustento teórico al pensamiento complejo cuyo objetivo es impulsar el desarrollo de altas capacidades y ofrecer escenarios formativos vinculados con el mundo real, y recursos para la innovación, la educación y la ciencia abierta.

El beneficio no solo será para estudiantes que hagan uso de la plataforma, sino también para personas de la academia y responsables de la toma de decisiones en diversas instituciones educativas. Colaboramos con empresas tecnológicas, ministerios de educación y trabajo, universidades, ONG y la sociedad en general para promover el aprendizaje continuo y el acceso universal al conocimiento. Este proyecto es crucial porque diversos estudios han demostrado que estimular y escalar el pensamiento complejo en las personas influye en el análisis, identificación y evaluación de sistemas complejos, generando nuevo conocimiento y fomentando el desarrollo de productos y procesos de emprendimiento.

¡Unámonos para aprovechar esta oportunidad y promover el emprendimiento social, científico y tecnológico, construyendo juntos un futuro lleno de innovación y aprendizaje continuo!

Nuestro objetivo es movilizar una plataforma educativa en línea que se beneficie del uso de las Tecnologías 5.0 e incremente los análisis y las propuestas desde el pensamiento complejo y el emprendimiento. Esta plataforma está diseñada para mejorar el rendimiento en competencias de pensamiento complejo en estudiantes de educación superior y personas en aprendizaje continuo. Utilizando escenarios de entrenamiento, herramientas tecnológicas y actividades modulares, fomentamos de manera accesible y asequible sub-competencias prioritarias como el pensamiento crítico, sistémico, innovador y científico. Al hacerlo, promovemos el desarrollo de soluciones creativas e innovadoras para problemas reales locales y globales, y estimulamos el emprendimiento basado en la tecnología en los ámbitos científico, tecnológico y social.

Objetivos específicos

1 Primero, diseñamos una plataforma en línea con funciones impulsadas por Tecnologías 5.0 para fomentar el emprendimiento científico, tecnológico y social mediante la formación en pensamiento complejo para estudiantes de educación superior y aprendices a lo largo de la vida.

2 Segundo, experimentamos, generamos y transferimos nuevo conocimiento a través de procesos de diseño, creación e implementación en diversos contextos educativos. Utilizamos métodos mixtos para obtener índices de rendimiento y resultados de evaluación que nos permiten medir el impacto en el desarrollo de habilidades de pensamiento complejo.

3 Tercero, creamos nuevos productos y servicios, generando la propiedad intelectual de la plataforma Educación 5.0, incluyendo la plataforma tecnológica, manuales, metodologías y programas de enseñanza-aprendizaje. Buscamos promover la transferencia de estos recursos a otras instituciones de educación superior, empresas educativas basadas en tecnología y entidades con objetivos alineados a nuestro proyecto.

Figura 2.
Objetivos generales y específicos de la plataforma OpenEdR4C

Objetivos

Introducción

¿Cómo potenciar las competencias de cada adulto en formación hacia el desarrollo de capacidades para el emprendimiento del presente y la construcción del futuro que queremos?

Sabemos que nuestra sociedad enfrenta retos cada vez más urgentes, entre otros, el cambio climático, el acceso a la educación de calidad y el empleo digno para fortalecer familias y comunidades. Los grandes problemas que aquejan al mundo y que nos obligan a tomar decisiones y acciones hacia una transformación social, nos colocan también frente a la necesidad de formarnos de una manera diferente. Estamos convencidos de que el camino que nos permita la búsqueda diferenciada de los desafíos que nos presenta el siglo XXI es el pensamiento complejo. Esta es una mega competencia que permite la interconexión de saberes y experiencias para visualizar posibilidades, innovar en las soluciones y ponerlas a prueba de forma rigurosa y sistemática en una sociedad en constante cambio. El desarrollo de esta competencia es fundamental para ser conscientes de la complejidad de las problemáticas y las implicaciones de las soluciones (Morin y Pakman, 2003), así como de los recursos disponibles para llegar a ellas de formas innovadoras, basadas en conocimiento y desarrollo tecnológico.

Si bien, el panorama para desarrollar propuestas de emprendimiento en todo el mundo es muy diverso, para quienes desean emprender en países emergentes, los retos que se les presentan deben partir de las especificidades propias de cada región y las necesidades emergentes. Según Mageste et al. (2024), un factor determinante es el desarrollo de las capacidades técnicas o de habilidades para poner en marcha proyectos rentables y económicamente sostenibles a través del tiempo. Por fortuna, las condiciones están dadas para ello, por ejemplo, en la región de América Latina y el Caribe tendrán un crecimiento en promedio de

2,1 % en el 2024, siendo este crecimiento para América del Sur un 1,6 %, para América Central y México un 2,7 % y El Caribe (excluyendo Guyana) un 2,8 % (CEPAL, 2024). El desafío que se presenta ahora es la construcción de un mayor crecimiento, más dinámico e inclusivo.

Como respuesta a este reto surge el proyecto OpenEdR4C con la visión de ofrecer una solución de alto impacto para resolver problemas en la educación y la sociedad a través del aprendizaje efectivo y autogestionado del emprendimiento (Figura 3). Este proyecto promueve una plataforma educativa abierta para coadyuvar con la formación de estudiantes universitarios y adultos en formación a lo largo de la vida y que deseen desarrollar su competencia de pensamiento complejo. Además, a través de la mejora de habilidades sobre emprendimiento social, científico y tecnológico, la plataforma ofrece la posibilidad de aportar soluciones a los Objetivos de Desarrollo Sostenible (ODS) (UNESCO, 2016), a través de proyectos de emprendimiento conectados con los contextos particulares de cada participante, mientras se conserva una visión global del impacto y la relevancia de cada proyecto.

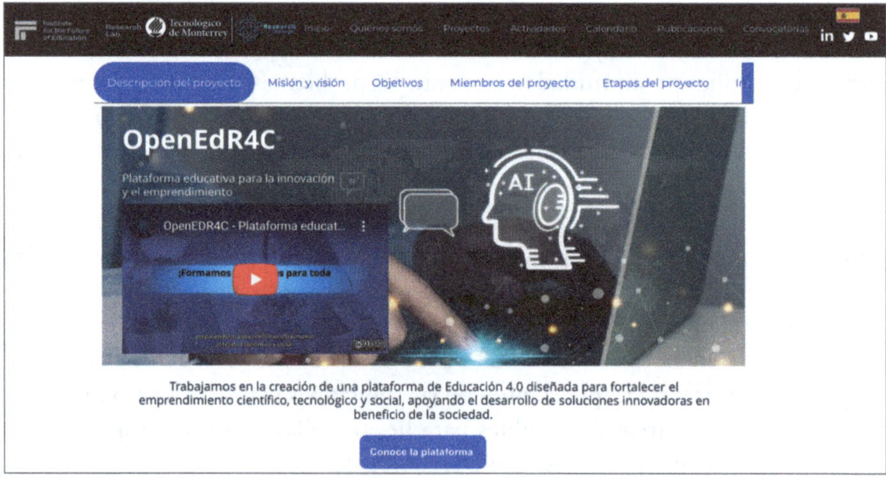

Figura 3. Página web del proyecto OpenEdR4C (https://www.research4challenges.world/openedr4c)

La plataforma OpenEDR4C (Figura 4) permite a las personas interesadas incrementar su conocimiento y las capacidades para la creación de empresas, con ideas innovadoras, basadas en la ciencia, la tecnología, el beneficio social y con compromiso ambiental. El contenido educativo de esta plataforma está diseñado para que diferentes perfiles de participantes encuentren recursos relevantes, que conecten con su entorno y les permita encontrar los caminos que conduzcan a las soluciones en espacios específicos. Teniendo en cuenta la diversidad, se ha incluido en la plataforma una herramienta que permite la atención a la neurodiversidad y a la diversidad sensorial, adecuando las características de la interfaz a las preferencias de cada persona.

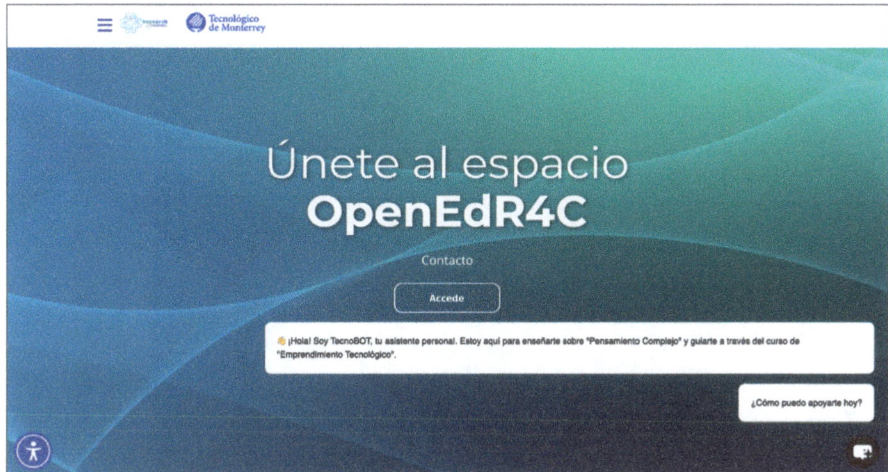

Figura 4. Plataforma OpenEdR4C (https://openedr4c.world)

Finalmente, los recursos (disponibles para descarga libre) atienden a los diferentes estilos de aprendizaje, ofreciendo diferentes medios para reforzar el conocimiento y desarrollar las subcompetencias del pensamiento complejo. Este recurso educativo abierto es una aportación para un nuevo ecosistema digital, en el que todas las personas tienen a su alcance recursos de calidad para atender a los retos de un mundo complejo y en constante cambio. Dirijamos ese cambio hacia el futuro que deseamos para que sea justo, equitativo, saludable y solidario.

Referencias

Morin, E. y Pakman, M. (2003). *Introducción al pensamiento complejo.* Barcelona: Gedisa.

Mageste, S., Plottier, C., Rocha, C. y Saporito, N. (2024). *Empresas emergentes (start-ups) en América Latina y el Caribe: una primera aproximación a su identificación y características.* Documentos de Proyectos (LC/TS.2023/179), Santiago, Comisión Económica para América Latina y el Caribe (CEPAL). https://repositorio.cepal.org/server/api/core/bitstreams/278c3c03-ec4a-4cea-a33c-20c08a30b4ef/content

CEPAL (2024). *Economías de América Latina y el Caribe crecerán 2,1% en 2024, en un contexto de incertidumbre a nivel global.* https://www.cepal.org/es/comunicados/economias-america-latina-caribe-creceran-21-2024-un-contexto-incertidumbre-nivel-global

UNESCO (2016). *Objetivos de Desarrollo Sostenible.* https://es.unesco.org/sdgs

¿Cómo se Vincula el Pensamiento Complejo con el Emprendimiento?

El pensamiento complejo es una forma de observar e interpretar la realidad, que reconoce y aborda la interconexión y la multiplicidad de factores presentes en diversas situaciones. En lugar de simplificar la realidad ("lo que se observa") en partes más pequeñas y analizarlas una por una, el pensamiento complejo nos invita a ver las situaciones en su totalidad, considerando cómo los elementos se influyen y se relacionan entre sí de maneras que a menudo son inesperadas. Esta aproximación es particularmente útil en tiempos de gran incertidumbre o cuando enfrentamos problemas que no tienen respuestas fáciles, como el fenómeno del cambio climático o las crisis económicas. Al adoptar un enfoque de pensamiento complejo, seremos capaces de apreciar de manera general y objetiva, la diversidad y las dinámicas que conforman "la realidad total", permitiéndonos tomar decisiones más informadas y efectivas.

El emprendimiento de tipo social, científico y/o tecnológico está profundamente vinculado con el desarrollo del pensamiento complejo, con competencias que abarcan el pensamiento sistémico, científico, innovador y crítico. Según un estudio realizado por Vázquez-Parra et al. (2022), se aplicó el instrumento validado eComplexity (Castillo-Martínez y Ramírez-Montoya, 2022) a 370 estudiantes de pregrado de diversas disciplinas, mostrando que las áreas de ingeniería, negocios y humanidades destacan en pensamiento sistémico, mientras que los estudiantes de Arquitectura se destacan en pensamiento crítico. En otro estudio exploratorio desarrollado por Ibarra-Vásquez et al. (2023), se analizó cómo el pensamiento complejo influye en el emprendimiento social, utilizando datos de 47 estudiantes y los resultados indican que, aunque las experiencias familiares previas no influyen directamente en el desarrollo de competencias de pensamiento complejo, sí ayudan a los estudiantes a familiarizarse con temas relacionados con el emprendimiento. Esto demuestra que el pensamiento complejo es esencial para enfrentar

PARA SABER MÁS....
sobre pensamiento complejo y su vinculación con el emprendimiento

Cambiemos de vía: lecciones de la pandemia

Autor: Edgar Morin

Referencia: Morin, E. (2020). *Cambiemos de vía: lecciones de la pandemia.* Paidós.

▶ Si quieres vincular el pensamiento complejo con el emprendimiento te recomendamos la obra de Morin, en donde se destaca la importancia de abordar la realidad considerando la interconexión y la influencia mutua de todos sus componentes, un enfoque especialmente relevante en tiempos de crisis como la pandemia de COVID-19. Esta visión nos enseña que, para generar soluciones innovadoras y sostenibles, debemos integrar distintas dimensiones del pensamiento complejo en nuestras iniciativas. Aplicar el pensamiento complejo nos permite enfrentar desafíos globales con una perspectiva holística, fomentando la creación de proyectos que no solo aborden problemas inmediatos, sino que también contribuyan al bienestar a largo plazo.

Social entrepreneurship and complex thinking. Validation of methodology for the scaling of the perception of competence achievement

Autores: José Carlos Vázquez-Parra, Martina Carlos-Arroyo y Marco Cruz-Sandoval

Referencia: Vázquez-Parra, J. C., Carlos-Arroyo, M. y Cruz-Sandoval, M. (2023). Social entrepreneurship and complex thinking. Validation of methodology for the scaling of the perception of competence achievement. *Ed.Sc. 13*(2). https://doi.org/10.3390/educsci13020186 https://hdl.handle.net/11285/650172

▶ Si quieres saber más sobre el pensamiento complejo y el emprendimiento, te recomendamos leer sobre la metodología SEL4C (Aprendizaje de Emprendimiento Social para la Complejidad), desarrollada por el Grupo de Investigación Interdisciplinaria Razonamiento para la Complejidad en el Instituto para el Futuro de la Educación del Tecnológico de Monterrey. Este artículo presenta un análisis estadístico de una intervención educativa realizada con estudiantes de una universidad mexicana, mostrando cómo esta metodología no solo mejora las competencias de emprendimiento social, sino que también desarrolla el pensamiento complejo. Los resultados validan que esta metodología es efectiva para formar competencias transversales esenciales en el mundo moderno. Juntos, podemos aprender a aplicar estas herramientas para enfrentar desafíos globales y contribuir al desarrollo sostenible.

Modelo abierto de pensamiento complejo para el futuro de la educación

Autores: María Soledad Ramírez- Montoya, Fabián Eduardo Basabe, Martina Carlos Arroyo, Irma Azeneth Patiño Zúñiga y May Portuguez Castro

Referencia: Ramírez-Montoya, M. S., Basabe, F. E., Carlos Arroyo, M., Patiño Zúñiga, I. A. y Portuguez Castro, M. (2024). *Modelo abierto de pensamiento complejo para el futuro de la educación.* Octaedro. https://hdl.handle.net/11285/652033

▶ Para descubrir más sobre pensamiento complejo, te invitamos a explorar un enfoque educativo innovador que se presenta en este texto. Este enfoque está diseñado para responder a las demandas del mundo moderno, integrando diversas dimensiones del pensamiento —crítico, científico, sistémico e innovador—. El objetivo es formar ciudadanos empáticos y comprometidos con el desarrollo sostenible. Este modelo no solo se aplica en ambientes académicos, sino también en sectores gubernamentales y empresariales, destacando la importancia de la colaboración, la empatía y el compromiso con soluciones sostenibles a problemas globales. Al sumergirte en este enfoque, podrás desarrollar habilidades que te permitirán contribuir de manera significativa a la sociedad y al bienestar del planeta.

los desafíos globales y generar valor social, contribuir con la innovación y con el progreso sostenible en nuestra sociedad.

La competencia de pensamiento complejo es fundamental para el desarrollo de emprendimientos exitosos, ya que permite a las personas emprendedoras aceptar la incertidumbre y acercarse a un profundo análisis de las características complejas del mundo empresarial moderno. Al abordar un proyecto empresarial con un enfoque de pensamiento complejo, las personas emprendedoras pueden identificar mejor las interconexiones entre diferentes áreas del mercado, anticipar posibles desafíos y oportunidades, y adaptar sus estrategias en consecuencia. Esta capacidad de análisis integradora y de adaptación es crucial para innovar y mantener la competitividad en un entorno económico dinámico y en constante evolución. Así, el pensamiento complejo no solo permite un mejoramiento en la toma de decisiones y la resolución de problemas, sino que también impulsa la capacidad de las personas emprendedoras para crear modelos de negocio más robustos y sostenibles.

Referencias

Castillo-Martínez, I. M. y Ramírez-Montoya, M. S. (2022). Instrumento eComplexity: Medición de la percepción de estudiantes de educación superior acerca de su competencia de razonamiento para la complejidad. https://hdl.handle.net/11285/643622

Ibarra-Vázquez, G., Ramírez-Montoya, M. S. y Miranda, J. (2023). Data Analysis in Factors of Social Entrepreneurship to Design Planning Tools in Complex Thinking. *Thinking Skills and Creativity 40*, 101381. https://doi.org/10.1016/j.tsc.2023.101381 https://hdl.handle.net/11285/651110

Vázquez-Parra, J. C.; Castillo-Martínez, I. M.; Ramírez-Montoya, M. S. y Millán, A. (2022). Development of the perception of achievement of complex thinking: A disciplinary approach in a Latin American student population. *Education Sciences 12*, Art. 289. https://doi.org/10.3390/educsci12050289

Innovación Educativa en Acción

La innovación en la educación abierta permite el acceso libre y gratuito a recursos de aprendizaje, rompiendo barreras económicas y geográficas. La plataforma OpenEDR4C es un recurso educativo abierto, esto quiere decir que puede ser usado sin la necesidad de realizar un pago para acceder a sus contenidos. Está diseñada para ofrecer una experiencia formativa autogestiva y retadora, facilitando el avance en cada uno de los temas y secciones de acuerdo con el ritmo de cada participante. El contenido de cada curso se diseñó de acuerdo con el modelo educativo abierto para el pensamiento complejo (Ramírez-Montoya et al., 2024), utilizando una estructura muy particular que combina los enfoques que fomentan el desarrollo de la competencia de pensamiento complejo, con contenido que estimula el espíritu empresarial para contribuir a los Objetivos de Desarrollo Sostenible (ODS). Adicionalmente, se integran en la plataforma diferentes herramientas y estrategias de aprendizaje que permiten una experiencia formativa integral y estimulante.

Al ser una plataforma autogestiva, se incluyeron herramientas de colaboración asincrónica entre participantes, por ejemplo, los foros de discusión donde es posible conocer las preocupaciones de otras personas trabajando sobre un mismo tema desde un contexto o país diferente. Del mismo modo, se promueve que cada participante utilice herramientas potenciadas por inteligencia artificial, a través de un chatbot que ofrece su ayuda mediante información y conceptos básicos sobre emprendimiento y sobre pensamiento complejo. Adicionalmente, se han integrado estrategias de visualización de escenarios, definición de elementos relevantes a considerar y para la presentación de videos. Todo ello permite a cada participante, avanzar en la construcción de propuestas de emprendimiento con una definición adecuada para convertir sus ideas en realidad.

La plataforma permite participar desde diferentes roles: estudiante, docente y administración. Desde el acceso con el rol de estudiantes se ingresa a los cursos en los tres niveles de avance en cada tema, básico, intermedio y avanzado. Para iniciar con cada curso, la plataforma solicitará un registro y el llenado de un perfil de persona usuaria como primera tarea a completar. Con esa información la plataforma permite la elaboración de informes para monitorear el avance de cada participante. Una vez que cada participante completa el perfil, se le solicita completar una prueba de diagnóstico antes de darle acceso a los cursos.

Con el rol docente se pueden crear grupos y elaborar informes sobre el rendimiento de cada estudiante, la realización de cursos, cuestionarios y pruebas. Con esta funcionalidad, cada docente puede monitorear el avance de sus grupos y conocer las necesidades de sus estudiantes para sugerir rutas diferenciadas, en atención a su ritmo de aprendizaje. Los grupos se crean asignando un curso y los niveles adecuados para cada participante (introductorio, intermedio o avanzado). Los reportes se podrán descargar a partir de los grupos o por cada curso que se haya seleccionado, con un rango de fecha establecido en la creación de los grupos.

Por otro lado, el rol de administración tiene atributos específicos: una persona administradora puede asignar roles a cada persona usuaria, crear grupos, gestionar todos los grupos y descargar informes generales. La administración de la plataforma está a cargo del grupo de investigación Escalando el Pensamiento Complejo para todos del Instituto para el futuro de la Educación del Tecnológico de Monterrey. El seguimiento desde este rol permite que cada persona investigadora a cargo utilice la información generada en la plataforma para desarrollar conocimiento acerca de las mejores y más efectivas formas para desarrollar el pensamiento complejo en las comunidades.

La página "Cursos" muestra las áreas asignadas a cada grupo, donde cada uno tiene una página de bienvenida que muestra detalles generales sobre el curso: la introducción, el objetivo, el tiempo aproximado para completar el curso, así como la autoría del contenido. Los cursos constan de cuatro temas con cuatro recursos cada uno. Cuestionarios y actividades adicionales complementan la experiencia educativa y la plataforma ofrece la libertad de desplazarse entre los contenidos, lo que permite a cada participante comprobar, revisar, repetir y conectar la información. Todos los recursos de la plataforma son recursos educativos abiertos (REA), protegidos por una licencia Creative Common para que puedan ser utilizados fuera del contexto de la plataforma. Existen videos con subtítulos que pueden verse en la plataforma o en YouTube. También hay cuestionarios con retroalimentación instantánea que se proporciona tras finalizar la prueba. Algunas actividades se realizan sin validación para ser reflexivas, mientras que otras son colaborativas y presentan la oportunidad de interactuar con las ideas de otras personas participantes. También se puede colaborar con otras personas a través del foro de discusión y con agentes de inteligencia artificial (IA) a través del chatbot. Este ente virtual está entrenado para proporcionar respuestas relacionadas con el tema; actualmente no es IA generativa, aunque en estos momentos se está diseñando una estrategia para proporcionar *feedback* sobre las actividades creativas.

Referencia

Ramírez-Montoya, M. S., Basabe, F. E., Carlos Arroyo, M., Patiño Zúñiga, I. A., Portuguez Castro, M. (2024). *Modelo abierto de pensamiento complejo para el futuro de la educación*. Octaedro. <https://hdl.handle.net/11285/652033>.

¿QUÉ DICEN LOS ESTUDIOS?

Sobre la propuesta que se realiza desde el proyecto de innovación

Promover el emprendimiento científico, social y tecnológico es esencial en la educación superior para preparar a cada estudiante para los desafíos del presente y del futuro. Necesitamos un contexto digital innovador y motivante, a través de una plataforma diseñada especialmente para ayudarte a desarrollar tus capacidades en estas áreas. Esta herramienta de innovación educativa no solo te enseña los fundamentos del emprendimiento, sino que también te ayuda a dominar el pensamiento complejo y sus componentes: pensamiento sistémico, creativo, innovador y científico. Al usar esta plataforma estarías aprendiendo no solo componentes teóricos, sino también aplicando estos principios y teorías a proyectos reales que pueden tener un impacto significativo en tu comunidad, considerando siempre los objetivos de desarrollo sustentables para ello.

De esta manera, se observa que el emprendimiento científico te permite transformar descubrimientos e ideas desde la ciencia, en soluciones prácticas que pueden mejorar tu entorno personal, familiar y social. Con esta plataforma, podrías aprender a identificar problemas científicos y desarrollar proyectos innovadores. Además, el desarrollo del pensamiento sistémico te ayuda a comprender cómo estos problemas se conectan con otros aspectos de la sociedad, cómo forman parte de un todo y te permiten crear soluciones completas, alcanzables y efectivas (George-Reyes et al., 2023). Al combinar esto con el pensamiento creativo y científico, estarías bien equipado para llevar tus ideas de un aula, de un laboratorio o de un contexto académico, hacia el mundo real.

Por otro lado, el emprendimiento social y tecnológico no solo consiste en crear nuevos productos usando la tecnología actual u ofrecer nuevos servicios de la sociedad, sino que trata de generar un impacto positivo que sea eficiente, productivo e inmediato. Esta plataforma educativa ayuda a pensar de manera innovadora, a desarrollar proyectos que aborden problemas sociales importantes utilizando la tecnología y a tomar consciencia de que es posible hacerlo. El pensamiento complejo, que incluye el pensamiento sistémico, creativo e innovador, te permite ver un panorama completo, real y encontrar soluciones que funcionen de manera eficiente y sustentable (Ramírez-Montoya et al., 2022). Si participas en este desarrollo, se logran promover nuevas formas de emprendimiento y nuevas maneras de contribuir a un mundo cada vez más necesitado de soluciones adecuadas, utilizando tus habilidades y conocimientos para hacer una diferencia significativa en tu entorno inmediato.

Referencia

George-Reyes, C., López-Caudana, E., y Lavonen, J. (2023). Complex and Design Thinking: Proof-of-Concept to Validate the i4C Methodology for Improving Scientific Entrepreneurship Skills. *Onomázein* (62),148–168. http://www.onomazein.com/index.php/onom/article/view/212 https://hdl.handle.net/11285/651470

Ramírez-Montoya, M. S., Castillo-Martínez, I.M., Sanabria-Zepeda, J.C. y Miranda, J. (2022). Complex Thinking in the Framework of Education 4.0 and Open Innovation—A Systematic Literature Review. *Journal of Open Innovation: Technology, Market, and Complexity 8*(4). https://doi.org/10.3390/joitmc8010004 https://repositorio.tec.mx/handle/11285/643380

TE INVITAMOS A REFLEXIONAR ...

¿Cómo crees que el emprendimiento social puede cambiar la manera en que abordamos los problemas más grandes del mundo, como la pobreza, la escasez de agua o el cambio climático?

___

___

___

¿Por qué piensas que es importante combinar la ciencia y la tecnología con el espíritu emprendedor?

___

___

___

Si tuvieras la oportunidad de crear una *startup* con base científica, social o tecnológica, ¿cuál sería tu enfoque principal? ¿Qué impacto esperarías lograr con tu emprendimiento?

___

___

___

ODS en la Educación

En el marco de los Objetivos de Desarrollo Sostenible (ODS), de manera particular la plataforma OpenEDR4C contribuye significativamente con el ODS 4, que busca garantizar una educación inclusiva, equitativa y de calidad, promoviendo oportunidades de aprendizaje durante toda la vida para todos. Al proporcionar recursos educativos abiertos y herramientas para el desarrollo de habilidades complejas, OpenEDR4C facilita el acceso a una educación de alta calidad, especialmente en áreas que tradicionalmente han sido desatendidas. Esto no solo mejora la calidad de la educación, sino que también democratiza el acceso al conocimiento, permitiendo que estudiantes de diversos espacios geográficos y contextos socioeconómicos tengan la posibilidad de acceder a las mismas oportunidades de aprendizaje.

Figura 5. ODS movilizados a través de la plataforma OpenEdR4C

Además del ODS 4, OpenEDR4C apoya los ODS 5 y 10 (Figura 5), que se centran en la igualdad de género y la reducción de las desigualdades, respectivamente. La plataforma promueve un entorno inclusivo que alienta la participación de mujeres y grupos vulnerables en el ámbito educativo y en la esfera del emprendimiento científico. Al ofrecer recursos y herramientas accesibles, OpenEDR4C ayuda a cerrar la brecha de género en la educación y fomenta la igualdad de oportunidades, independientemente del género, etnia o nivel socioeconómico. De esta manera, la plataforma no solo empodera a las mujeres y otros grupos marginados, sino que también contribuye a una sociedad más equitativa y justa, alineada con los principios de los ODS.

Referencia

UNESCO (2016). *Objetivos de Desarrollo Sostenible.* https://es.unesco.org/sdgs

PARA SABER MÁS ...
el vínculo entre los ODS y la propuesta

Exploring entrepreneurship related to the sustainable development goals - mapping new venture activities with semi-automated content analysis

Autores: Jannic Horne, Malte Recker, Ingo Michelfelder, Jason Jay y Jan Kratzer

Referencia: Horne, J., Recker, M., Michelfelder, I., Jay, J., y Kratzer, J. (2020). Exploring entrepreneurship related to the sustainable development goals - mapping new venture activities with semi-automated content analysis. *Journal of Cleaner Production*, 242, 118052.

▶ Para descubrir más sobre los Objetivos de Desarrollo Sostenible (ODS) y el emprendimiento, te invitamos a explorar estudios como esta propuesta, en la cual se analiza cómo el emprendimiento en Alemania contribuye a los ODS. Utilizando un análisis de contenido semiautomatizado, los autores de este estudio han mapeado las actividades de nuevas empresas en relación con los ODS, identificando patrones y áreas de oportunidad donde el emprendimiento puede tener un impacto significativo en el cumplimiento de estos objetivos. Al profundizar en este tipo de investigaciones, no solo aprenderás cómo las iniciativas empresariales pueden apoyar el desarrollo sostenible, sino que también podrás identificar maneras en las que tú mismo puedes contribuir a un futuro más sostenible y equitativo.

Engagement and Social Impact in Tech-Based Citizen Science Initiatives for Achieving the SDGs: A Systematic Literature Review with a Perspective on Complex Thinking

Autores: Jorge Sanabria-Z, Berenice Alfaro-Ponce, Omar Israel González Peña, Hugo Terashima-Marín y José Carlos Ortiz-Bayliss

Referencia: Sanabria-Z, J., Alfaro-Ponce, B., González Peña, O. I., Terashima-Marín, H. y Ortiz-Bayliss, J. C. (2022). Engagement and Social Impact in Tech-Based Citizen Science Initiatives for Achieving the SDGs: A Systematic Literature Review with a Perspective on Complex Thinking. *Sustainability 14*(17), 10978. https://doi.org/10.3390/su141710978 https://repositorio.tec.mx/handle/11285/648805

▶ Para aprender más sobre el pensamiento complejo, los ODS y el emprendimiento, te recomendamos explorar los avances en proyectos de ciencia ciudadana. Estos proyectos, que han progresado significativamente en los últimos años, abordan desafíos globales complejos y apoyan la agenda 2030 de los ODS. La UNESCO destaca que la ciencia ciudadana puede cerrar brechas en ciencia, tecnología e innovación, acercando a la gente común a estos campos. Un estudio reciente revisó 49 proyectos de ciencia ciudadana y encontró que, aunque estos proyectos se implementan ampliamente en Europa y se centran en temas como el entorno construido y la monitorización ambiental, todavía hay una gran oportunidad para desarrollar tecnologías nativas y aumentar la participación ciudadana. Esto no solo logra un mayor impacto social, sino que también fomenta el desarrollo de habilidades de pensamiento complejo en los participantes. Te invitamos a unirte a estas iniciativas, que no solo benefician a la comunidad, sino que también te ayudarán a mejorar tu capacidad de análisis y resolución de problemas complejos.

Nuevos Escenarios Educativos

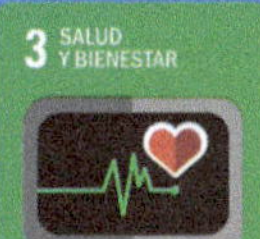

ESCENARIO EDUCATIVO dirigido a estudiantes

Conoce el Emprendimiento científico en la plataforma OpenEDR4C: ecosistema del emprendimiento científico

ODS vinculados

Actividad

En esta actividad, explorarás el concepto de emprendimiento científico utilizando la plataforma OpenEDR4C. Aprenderás cómo el conocimiento científico puede contribuir a la transformación de las empresas haciéndolas innovadoras, que contribuyan al desarrollo tecnológico y favorezcan la resolución de problemas locales y globales. A lo largo de esta experiencia, descubrirás el ecosistema digital de OpenEDR4C que fomenta la comprensión del emprendimiento científico.

Objetivo

Identificar y desarrollar oportunidades de emprendimiento científico, utilizando el ecosistema de la plataforma OpenEDR4C para apoyar cada etapa del proceso, desde la generación de ideas hasta la presentación de proyectos empresariales.

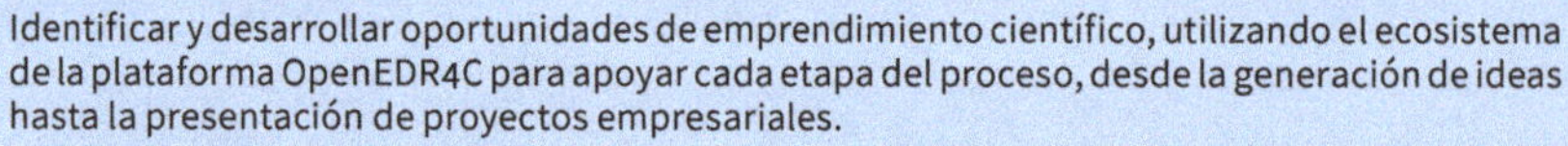

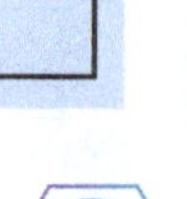

Inicio

1. Regístrate en OpenEDR4C y realiza una evaluación diagnóstica para conocer tus competencias en pensamiento complejo y emprendimiento.
2. Observa el video de bienvenida que explica los objetivos del curso y cómo navegar por la plataforma para aprovechar al máximo los contenidos y herramientas interactivas.

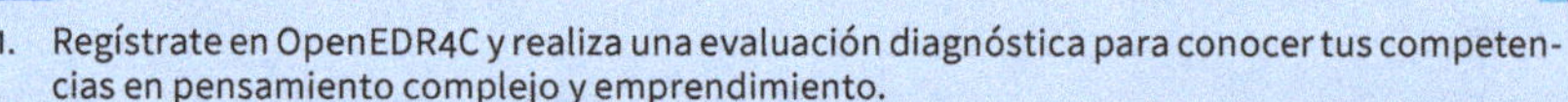

Desarrollo

Accederás a talleres y actividades que te enseñarán cómo evaluar ideas científicas por su potencial comercial, cómo desarrollar modelos de negocio y cómo comunicar efectivamente tus ideas a inversores y *stakeholders*. Estos talleres incluyen ejercicios prácticos en la plataforma, donde podrás aplicar lo aprendido en un entorno controlado.

Utilizando las herramientas de desarrollo en línea de OpenEDR4C, trabajarás en la elaboración de tu idea de negocio. La plataforma facilita la interacción en tiempo real y la gestión de proyectos, permitiéndote compartir documentos, dar y recibir *feedback* y actualizar tus progresos.

A lo largo del curso, completarás las evaluaciones formativas que te ayudarán a monitorear tu progreso e identificar áreas de mejora. Estas evaluaciones están integradas en la plataforma y son fundamentales para asegurar que alcances los objetivos de aprendizaje establecidos.

Cierre

Al final del curso, entregarás un proyecto que será evaluado utilizando una rúbrica de emprendimiento científico. Recibirás retroalimentación detallada que podrás utilizar para mejorar tus propuestas o prepararte para futuras oportunidades de emprendimiento.

Cada participante que complete satisfactoriamente todas las partes del curso recibirá un certificado digital a través de la plataforma, reconociendo su participación y el logro de los objetivos.

Evaluación

El proceso de evaluación se llevará a cabo de diversas formas:

- Evaluaciones formativas: durante el desarrollo de la actividad, se realizarán evaluaciones periódicas dentro de la plataforma, así como autoevaluaciones. Estas evaluaciones te permitirán recibir retroalimentación inmediata sobre tu progreso y entender mejor los conceptos clave del emprendimiento científico.
- Cuestionarios para evaluar el desarrollo de competencias: se utilizarán cuestionarios de percepción para medir el desarrollo de competencias en pensamiento complejo y emprendimiento.
- Rúbrica de emprendimiento científico: la rúbrica considera 4 dimensiones de análisis —colaboración, conocimiento, diseño de proyectos y habilidades para la investigación—. Evalúa las habilidades de emprendimiento desarrolladas por cada estudiante.

Evidencia de Aprendizaje

Para evidenciar tu participación, se tomarán los registros de actividad en la plataforma OpenEDR4C, las respuestas a los cuestionarios de conocimientos y percepción, así como las actividades que deberás completar y entregar en la plataforma.

Materiales o Herramientas Digitales

Para realizar efectivamente la actividad en la plataforma OpenEDR4C, necesitarás:

- Acceso a OpenEDR4C: se logra fácilmente utilizando una cuenta de correo.
- Dispositivos móviles: puedes usar teléfonos inteligentes, *tablets*, *laptops* o computadoras de escritorio.
- Acceso a Internet: fundamental para participar en todas las actividades y utilizar las herramientas de la plataforma.

ESCENARIO EDUCATIVO dirigido a docentes

Escenario educativo para docentes en la plataforma OpenEDR4C: emprendimiento científico

ODS vinculados

Actividad

Esta actividad está diseñada para ti, docente, que explorarás la plataforma OpenEDR4C y el curso de emprendimiento científico. En esta experiencia aprenderás cómo el conocimiento científico puede contribuir a la transformación de las empresas haciéndolas innovadoras, que contribuyan al desarrollo tecnológico y favorezcan la resolución de problemas locales y globales. Conocerás el ecosistema digital de OpenEDR4C, que te ayudará a comprender qué es el emprendimiento científico y cómo puedes guiar a cada estudiante en esta área de conocimiento.

Objetivo

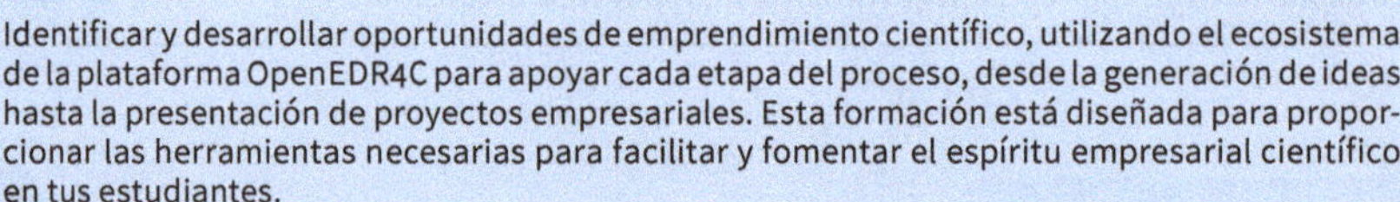

Identificar y desarrollar oportunidades de emprendimiento científico, utilizando el ecosistema de la plataforma OpenEDR4C para apoyar cada etapa del proceso, desde la generación de ideas hasta la presentación de proyectos empresariales. Esta formación está diseñada para proporcionar las herramientas necesarias para facilitar y fomentar el espíritu empresarial científico en tus estudiantes.

Inicio

1. Regístrate en OpenEDR4C y completa una evaluación diagnóstica inicial para medir tus competencias en pensamiento complejo y emprendimiento.
2. Observa el video de bienvenida que explica detalladamente los objetivos del curso y cómo puedes utilizar la plataforma para maximizar los beneficios de los contenidos y herramientas interactivas disponibles.

Desarrollo

Accederás a talleres diseñados para evaluar ideas científicas por su potencial comercial, desarrollar modelos de negocio efectivos y comunicar estas ideas de manera efectiva a inversores y otros interesados. Estos talleres incluyen ejercicios prácticos que te permitirán aplicar lo aprendido en un contexto controlado.

Utilizando las herramientas de OpenEDR4C, trabajarás en la elaboración de tus propias ideas de negocio. La plataforma facilita la interacción en tiempo real y la gestión de proyectos, permitiéndote compartir documentos, recibir y ofrecer retroalimentación, y monitorear tu progreso.

A lo largo del curso, realizarás evaluaciones formativas integradas en la plataforma, ayudándote a monitorear tu progreso e identificar áreas de mejora. Estas evaluaciones son cruciales para garantizar que alcances los objetivos de aprendizaje.

Cierre

Al final del curso, presentarás tu proyecto de emprendimiento científico, que será evaluado mediante una rúbrica diseñada para medir la viabilidad, innovación y potencial de impacto del proyecto. Recibirás retroalimentación detallada, fundamental para mejorar tus propuestas y prepararte para liderar futuras iniciativas de emprendimiento.

Cada docente que complete satisfactoriamente todas las etapas del curso recibirá un certificado digital a través de la plataforma, reconociendo su participación y logro de los objetivos. Este certificado te servirá como reconocimiento de tu capacidad para guiar y motivar a tus estudiantes en proyectos de emprendimiento científico.

Evaluación

Durante el desarrollo de la actividad, se realizarán evaluaciones periódicas que incluyen cuestionarios en línea y autoevaluaciones. Estas evaluaciones te permitirán recibir retroalimentación inmediata sobre tu progreso y entender mejor los conceptos clave del emprendimiento científico.

Se utilizarán cuestionarios de percepción para medir el desarrollo de competencias en pensamiento complejo y emprendimiento.

Evidencia de Aprendizaje

Para evidenciar la participación, se tomarán los registros de actividad en la plataforma OpenEDR4C, las respuestas a los cuestionarios de conocimientos y percepción, así como las actividades que deberán subir a la plataforma.

Materiales o Herramientas Digitales

Acceso a OpenEDR4C: se logra fácilmente utilizando una cuenta de correo.

- Dispositivos móviles: puedes usar teléfonos inteligentes, *tablets*, *laptops* o computadoras de escritorio.
- Acceso a Internet: fundamental para participar en todas las actividades y utilizar las herramientas de la plataforma.

ESCENARIO EDUCATIVO dirigido a empresas

Actividad de emprendimiento científico en la plataforma OpenEDR4C: orientada a empresas

ODS vinculados

Actividad

OpenEDR4C permite a las empresas explorar y expandir sus horizontes en el mundo del emprendimiento científico. Esta actividad está enfocada en cómo transformar el conocimiento científico en innovaciones comerciales que no solo impulsen el crecimiento empresarial, sino que también contribuyan a solucionar problemas locales y globales.

Objetivo

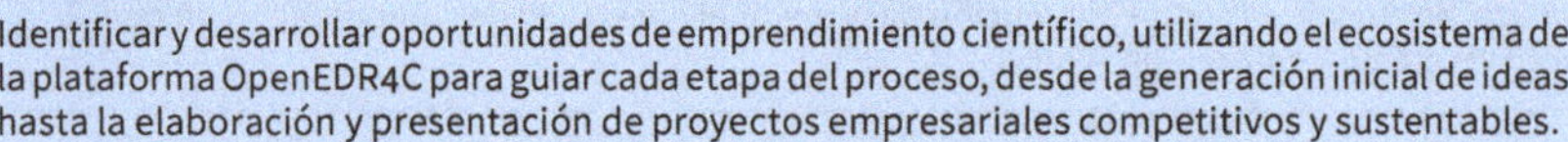

Identificar y desarrollar oportunidades de emprendimiento científico, utilizando el ecosistema de la plataforma OpenEDR4C para guiar cada etapa del proceso, desde la generación inicial de ideas hasta la elaboración y presentación de proyectos empresariales competitivos y sustentables.

Inicio

- Regístrate en OpenEDR4C y completa una evaluación diagnóstica inicial para mapear tus competencias actuales en pensamiento complejo y emprendimiento.
- Observa el video de bienvenida que explica detalladamente los objetivos del curso y proporciona una guía sobre cómo navegar por la plataforma, ayudándote a maximizar el uso de los contenidos y las herramientas interactivas.

Desarrollo

Tendrás acceso a talleres dirigidos por expertos, donde incrementarás habilidades para evaluar el potencial comercial de las ideas científicas, desarrollar modelos de negocio robustos y comunicar de manera efectiva tus ideas a inversores y otros *stakeholders* relevantes. Estos talleres incluyen ejercicios prácticos en la plataforma, facilitando la aplicación directa de los conocimientos adquiridos.

Utilizarás las herramientas de OpenEDR4C para trabajar en la formulación y refinamiento de tus propias ideas de negocio. La plataforma ofrece recursos para facilitar la interacción en tiempo real, la gestión de proyectos, compartir documentos, recibir y dar *feedback*, y monitorizar el progreso de manera continua.

Completarás evaluaciones formativas diseñadas para ayudarte a monitorear tu progreso e identificar áreas de mejora. Estas evaluaciones están integradas en la plataforma y son cruciales para garantizar que alcances los objetivos de aprendizaje establecidos.

Cierre

Al final del taller, presentarás tu proyecto de emprendimiento científico, que será evaluado según una rúbrica especializada en emprendimiento científico. Estas presentaciones te ofrecerán una oportunidad para recibir retroalimentación detallada, que podrás utilizar para perfeccionar tus propuestas o prepararte para futuras oportunidades.

Cada participante que complete satisfactoriamente todas las etapas del curso recibirá un certificado digital a través de la plataforma, reconociendo su participación activa y el cumplimiento de los objetivos. Este certificado puede servir como un diferenciador en el mercado, destacando tu compromiso con la innovación y el desarrollo continuo.

Evaluación

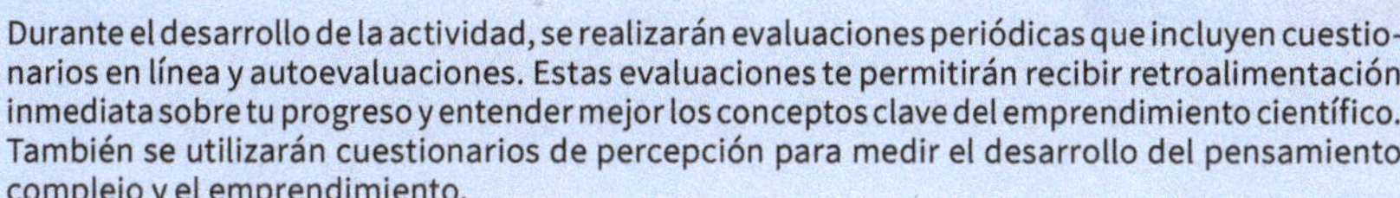

Durante el desarrollo de la actividad, se realizarán evaluaciones periódicas que incluyen cuestionarios en línea y autoevaluaciones. Estas evaluaciones te permitirán recibir retroalimentación inmediata sobre tu progreso y entender mejor los conceptos clave del emprendimiento científico. También se utilizarán cuestionarios de percepción para medir el desarrollo del pensamiento complejo y el emprendimiento.

Evidencia de Aprendizaje

Para evidenciar tu participación, se tomarán los registros de actividad en la plataforma OpenEDR4C, las respuestas a los cuestionarios de conocimientos y percepción, así como las actividades que se soliciten desde la plataforma.

Materiales o Herramientas Digitales

- Acceso a OpenEDR4C: se logra fácilmente utilizando una cuenta de correo.
- Dispositivos móviles: puedes usar teléfonos inteligentes, *tablets*, *laptops* o computadoras de escritorio.
- Acceso a Internet: fundamental para participar en todas las actividades y utilizar las herramientas de la plataforma.

ESCENARIO EDUCATIVO dirigido a ONG

Actividad de emprendimiento científico en la plataforma OpenEDR4C para ONG

ODS vinculados

Actividad

Esta experiencia está orientada a mostrar cómo el conocimiento científico puede transformarse en iniciativas innovadoras que no solo contribuyen al desarrollo tecnológico, sino que también abordan desafíos locales y globales. Durante esta actividad, explorarás la plataforma OpenEDR4C y descubrirás cómo tu organización puede generar un cambio positivo dando respuestas a las problemáticas sociales actuales.

Objetivo

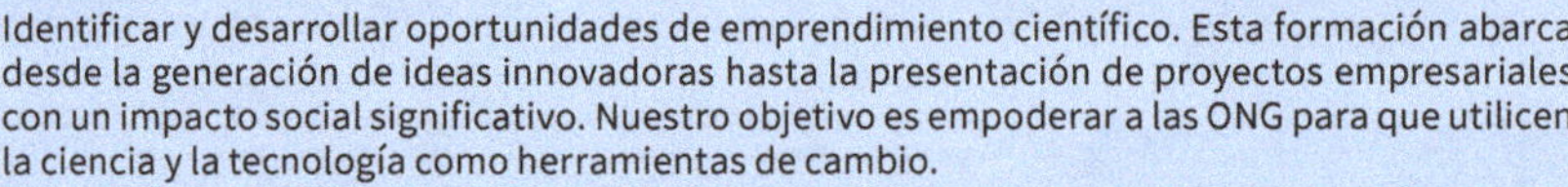

Identificar y desarrollar oportunidades de emprendimiento científico. Esta formación abarca desde la generación de ideas innovadoras hasta la presentación de proyectos empresariales con un impacto social significativo. Nuestro objetivo es empoderar a las ONG para que utilicen la ciencia y la tecnología como herramientas de cambio.

Inicio

- Regístrate en OpenEDR4C y realiza una evaluación diagnóstica para medir tus habilidades en pensamiento complejo y emprendimiento, lo cual es crucial para adaptar el curso a tus necesidades específicas.
- Revisa el video de bienvenida que explica detalladamente los objetivos del curso y te orienta sobre cómo navegar por la plataforma para aprovechar al máximo los contenidos educativos y las herramientas interactivas.

Desarrollo

Tendrás acceso a talleres donde aprenderás a evaluar ideas científicas por su potencial comercial y social, a desarrollar modelos de negocio sostenibles y a comunicar efectivamente tus ideas a inversores y personas interesadas clave. Estos talleres incluyen ejercicios prácticos en la plataforma, permitiéndote aplicar lo aprendido en un entorno controlado y colaborativo.

Utilizarás las herramientas de desarrollo en línea de OpenEDR4C para elaborar tus ideas de negocio. La plataforma facilita la interacción en tiempo real y la gestión de proyectos, permitiendo a las ONG compartir documentos, recibir y dar retroalimentación, y actualizar sus avances.

Completarás evaluaciones formativas a lo largo del curso para monitorear tu progreso e identificar áreas de mejora. Estas evaluaciones, integradas en la plataforma, son fundamentales para asegurar que alcances los objetivos de aprendizaje propuestos.

Cierre

Al final de la actividad, presentarás tu proyecto de emprendimiento científico, que será evaluado mediante una rúbrica enfocada en el impacto social y la viabilidad. Cada participante que complete satisfactoriamente todas las partes del curso recibirá un certificado digital a través de la plataforma, reconociendo su participación y el éxito en alcanzar los objetivos de aprendizaje.

Evaluación

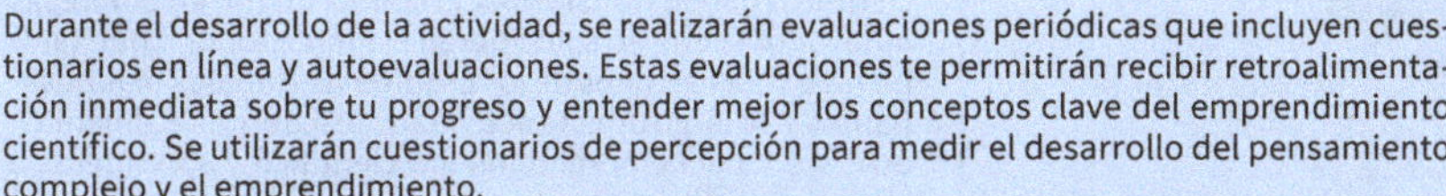

Durante el desarrollo de la actividad, se realizarán evaluaciones periódicas que incluyen cuestionarios en línea y autoevaluaciones. Estas evaluaciones te permitirán recibir retroalimentación inmediata sobre tu progreso y entender mejor los conceptos clave del emprendimiento científico. Se utilizarán cuestionarios de percepción para medir el desarrollo del pensamiento complejo y el emprendimiento.

Evidencia de Aprendizaje

Para evidenciar la implementación, se tomarán los registros de actividad de los usuarios en la plataforma OpenEDR4C, las respuestas a los cuestionarios de conocimientos y percepción, así como las actividades que se soliciten desde la plataforma.

Materiales o Herramientas Digitales

- Acceso a OpenEDR4C, que se logra muy fácilmente utilizando una cuenta de correo.
- Dispositivos móviles como teléfonos inteligentes o *tablets*, también pueden usarse *laptops* y computadoras de escritorio.
- Acceso a internet.

ESCENARIO EDUCATIVO dirigido a *lifelong learning*

Introducción a la actividad de emprendimiento científico en OpenEDR4C

ODS vinculados

Actividad

Bienvenido a esta experiencia educativa de la plataforma OpenEDR4C, diseñada especialmente para personas que están comprometidas con el aprendizaje continuo a lo largo de la vida. Aquí explorarás cómo el emprendimiento científico puede transformar el conocimiento en empresas innovadoras que no solo lideran el mercado, sino que también abordan algunos de los problemas globales más desafiantes. A lo largo de esta actividad, descubrirás el dinámico ecosistema del emprendimiento científico y aprenderás a integrarte activamente en este campo, sin importar en qué fase de tu carrera profesional te encuentres.

Objetivo

Identificar y desarrollar oportunidades de emprendimiento científico, utilizando la plataforma OpenEDR4C. Esta formación abarca desde la generación inicial de ideas hasta la presentación efectiva de proyectos empresariales.

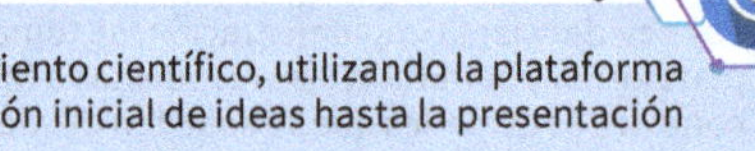

Inicio

- Regístrate en OpenEDR4C y completa una evaluación diagnóstica que personalizará tu experiencia de aprendizaje, ajustando los contenidos según tus competencias actuales en pensamiento complejo y emprendimiento.
- Revisa el video explicativo que te mostrará cómo navegar por la plataforma. Esto te ayudará a maximizar el aprovechamiento de los contenidos disponibles y de las herramientas interactivas, asegurando que puedas acceder fácilmente a todo lo necesario para tener éxito en el curso.

Desarrollo

Participarás en talleres diseñados para enseñarte a evaluar el potencial comercial de ideas científicas, a desarrollar modelos de negocio sólidos y a comunicar efectivamente tus ideas a potenciales inversores y otras partes interesadas.

Utilizarás las herramientas de desarrollo en línea de OpenEDR4C para elaborar tus ideas de negocio. La plataforma facilita la interacción en tiempo real y la gestión de proyectos, permitiéndote compartir documentos, recibir y dar retroalimentación, y seguir de cerca tus progresos.

Completa las evaluaciones integradas en la plataforma a lo largo del curso para monitorear tu progreso e identificar áreas de mejora. Estas evaluaciones son fundamentales para asegurar que alcances los objetivos de aprendizaje establecidos.

Cierre

Como actividad final, presentarás tu proyecto de emprendimiento científico, que será evaluado usando una rúbrica detallada. Las personas participantes que completen satisfactoriamente todas las partes del curso recibirán un certificado digital a través de la plataforma, reconociendo su participación activa y el logro de los objetivos.

Evaluación

Durante el desarrollo de la actividad, se realizarán evaluaciones periódicas que incluyen cuestionarios en línea y autoevaluaciones. Estas evaluaciones te permitirán recibir retroalimentación inmediata sobre tu progreso y entender mejor los conceptos clave del emprendimiento científico. Se utilizarán cuestionarios de percepción para medir el escalamiento del pensamiento complejo y el emprendimiento.

Evidencia de Aprendizaje

Para evidenciar la actividad, se tomarán los registros de los usuarios en la plataforma OpenEDR4C, las respuestas a los cuestionarios de conocimientos y percepción, así como las actividades solicitadas en la plataforma.

Materiales o Herramientas Digitales

- Acceso a OpenEDR4C: se logra fácilmente utilizando una cuenta de correo.
- Dispositivos móviles: teléfonos inteligentes o *tablets*, además de *laptops* y computadoras de escritorio.
- Acceso a Internet: fundamental para participar en todas las actividades y utilizar las herramientas de la plataforma.

1

Definir nuestras metas en el mediano y largo plazo, reconociendo nuestras capacidades y necesidades. Entender qué valor tiene la plataforma para nuestra comunidad, dependerá de definir cómo puede ayudarnos a cumplir nuestros objetivos individuales o colectivos. El rol que desempeñamos en el presente puede ser el punto de partida, pero es importante imaginar hacia dónde queremos llegar (definir las metas) y de qué forma las capacidades desarrollables en la plataforma pueden contribuir para ser alcanzadas.

2

Establecer un marco de referencia con los Objetivos de Desarrollo Sostenible. Cada uno de las personas participantes tendrá alguna prioridad, por ejemplo, cada estudiante querrá emprender en cuanto terminen sus estudios, por su parte el cuerpo docente, querrá contar con herramientas actualizadas y valiosas para sus cursos. Reconocer los problemas de nuestra comunidad que queremos resolver a través del desarrollo de ideas de emprendimiento, nos ayudará a dirigir nuestros esfuerzos.

3

Fijar un nivel de alcance de las propuestas de emprendimiento que se generarán en el curso. Esta definición nos llevará a proponer con mayor nivel de detalle, las soluciones que nos permitirán generar un cambio en nuestras sociedades. Para el caso de las personas adultas en formación, por ejemplo, el definir si llegarán a un producto mínimo viable o a una presentación para obtener inversión, establece dos rutas de acción complementarias, pero distintas.

4

Identificar a quiénes queremos beneficiar con nuestra propuesta, imaginando el futuro que queremos. En esta etapa es muy importante preguntarnos cómo incluir a diferentes grupos de personas que requieran beneficiarse de esta solución, pero además que pueden tener diferentes roles, por ejemplo, personas socias, licenciatarias, clientes, inversionistas, etc., las diferentes personas que representan diversos sectores de la sociedad que pueden beneficiarse con nuestra propuesta de emprendimiento.

5

Construcción de una propuesta de emprendimiento, a partir del conocimiento adquirido en las etapas previas. La intención es promover la búsqueda de soluciones innovadoras y la generación de propuestas que beneficien a la comunidad seleccionada de forma creativa y sostenible, ya sea a través del emprendimiento científico, tecnológico o social.

6

Evaluación de la experiencia formativa. La última fase de la implementación, se centrará en hacer una evaluación acerca de las capacidades desarrolladas durante la experiencia formativa. Por una lado, cada participante podrá hacer una autoevaluación de tipo reflexivo para determinar qué tanto le aportó la experiencia. Sin embargo para el grupo de docentes y personas capacitadoras, también podrán hacer uso de los reportes para revisar los avances de sus grupos en formación y tomar acciones para reforzar o continuar por una ruta exitosa.

Figura 6.
Recomendaciones para implementar la plataforma OpenEdR4C

Recomendaciones para la Implementación

La implementación de la plataforma OpenEDR4C será distinta para cada uno de los contextos en donde se adopte y de los roles de las personas participantes, ya sean estudiantes, docentes, empresas, adultos en formación a lo largo de su vida y quienes trabajen hacia la consecución de los Objetivos de Desarrollo Sostenible (ODS) desde diversos frentes de acción. Para cada sector, las recomendaciones de implementación tendrán diferentes enfoques, sin embargo, todas ellas se centran en la construcción de un escenario formativo en el que se considere el desarrollo de las cuatro sub-competencias del pensamiento complejo: pensamiento científico, crítico, sistémico e innovador. Pero ¿cómo podemos incluir estos elementos en escenarios que se puedan visualizar desde diferentes enfoques y que promuevan soluciones a los retos globales a partir del emprendimiento?

El siguiente listado te ayudará a establecer una pauta adecuada para la implementación de la plataforma OpenEdR4C en cada uno de los sectores relevantes (Figura 6).

Estudio de caso: emprendimiento para resolver el acceso a agua potable en comunidades rurales

En una comunidad rural, la falta de acceso al agua potable es un problema que afecta la salud y la calidad de vida de sus habitantes. Muchos deben caminar largas distancias para obtener agua de fuentes no seguras, lo que aumenta la incidencia de enfermedades y limita el tiempo para actividades productivas. En respuesta, un grupo de emprendedores decide desarrollar un proyecto que combina tecnología, ciencia y emprendimiento social para mejorar el acceso al agua potable.

El equipo de emprendimiento utiliza conocimientos científicos para desarrollar un sistema de purificación de agua asequible y adaptable a condiciones rurales. Este sistema emplea energía solar para funcionar de manera independiente, sin necesidad de una red eléctrica. Además, su diseño modular permite su adaptación a diferentes volúmenes de agua, lo cual es crucial en comunidades de tamaño variable.

Para implementar el proyecto, el grupo lanza una campaña de financiamiento colectivo, sensibilizando a personas e instituciones sobre la importancia de apoyar soluciones sostenibles para el acceso al agua. El objetivo es instalar este sistema en puntos estratégicos de la comunidad y capacitar a sus habitantes en su uso y mantenimiento, promoviendo así la autogestión y sostenibilidad del proyecto. Además, se exploran alianzas con ONG para ampliar el alcance del proyecto a otras comunidades en situación similar.

¿Cómo funciona la plataforma OpenEdR4c para resolver el caso?

La plataforma OpenEDR4C sigue un enfoque estructurado para resolver el caso. El proceso se explica a continuación:

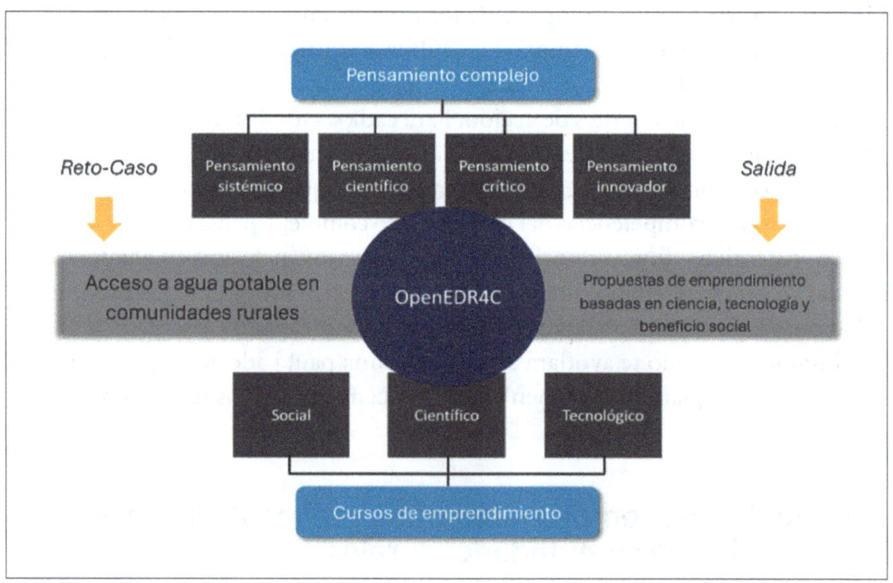

Reto-caso: el primer paso implica presentar un problema real o desafío, en este caso, el acceso al agua potable en comunidades rurales.

1. **Pensamiento complejo.** La plataforma fomenta diferentes sub-competencias de pensamiento complejo, que son claves para abordar problemas complejos:
   - **Pensamiento sistémico.** Permite analizar el caso desde una perspectiva holística, entendiendo las interconexiones entre los diversos factores que influyen en el acceso al agua potable.

- **Pensamiento científico.** Utiliza un enfoque basado en evidencia para investigar causas y posibles soluciones científicas.
- **Pensamiento crítico.** Se promueve la evaluación crítica de la información y las soluciones propuestas.
- **Pensamiento innovador.** Fomenta la generación de ideas novedosas para resolver el problema de manera creativa.

2. **OpenEDR4C como eje.** La plataforma integra estos tipos de pensamiento, sirviendo de núcleo central donde los usuarios (estudiantes o emprendedores) pueden trabajar en soluciones al reto planteado.
3. **Cursos de emprendimiento.** OpenEDR4C incluye cursos de emprendimiento en tres áreas fundamentales:
   - **Social:** para abordar el impacto social de las propuestas.
   - **Científico:** enfocado en soluciones fundamentadas en conocimientos científicos.
   - **Tecnológico:** orientado a la creación de soluciones tecnológicas para el problema.
4. **Salida - Propuestas de emprendimiento.** Finalmente, el objetivo es generar propuestas de emprendimiento que beneficien a la comunidad, utilizando enfoques de ciencia, tecnología y beneficios sociales. Estas propuestas representan una salida concreta y aplicable del trabajo realizado en la plataforma.

Preguntas de reflexión

Emprendimiento científico

¿Cuál de las siguientes es una estrategia adecuada para validar la efectividad del sistema de purificación de agua desarrollado en este caso?

a) Realizar pruebas en laboratorio y en condiciones de campo para evaluar su eficiencia y adaptabilidad. ☑
b) Utilizar únicamente modelos matemáticos para estimar su efectividad en campo.
c) Probar el sistema solo en condiciones de laboratorio sin considerar variables ambientales.

Emprendimiento social

¿Qué aspecto es fundamental en el emprendimiento social, según el enfoque de este caso?

a) Crear un producto que sea exclusivo para una minoría que pueda pagar.
b) Desarrollar soluciones que beneficien a la comunidad y contribuyan al bienestar social. ☑
c) Centrarse únicamente en maximizar los beneficios económicos de la empresa.

Emprendimiento tecnológico

¿Cuál es el enfoque adecuado para implementar una tecnología en un contexto rural como el descrito?

a) Usar tecnología avanzada sin considerar las necesidades y capacidades locales.
b) Desarrollar una tecnología que no requiera mantenimiento y pueda operar sin supervisión.
c) Implementar tecnología accesible y fácil de mantener, adaptada a la disponibilidad de recursos locales. ☑

RECURSOS EDUCATIVOS ABIERTOS (REA)

REA: Educational entrepreneurship—UNESCO chair open educational movement for LATAM 2023.
Autores: María Soledad Ramírez Montoya y Jhonattan Miranda Mendoza.
Referencia: Ramírez Montoya, M. S. y Miranda Mendoza, J. (2024). *Educational entrepreneurship—UNESCO chair open educational movement for LATAM 2023* [Video]. https://hdl.handle.net/11285/676164

Te invitamos a sumergirte en un inspirador recurso educativo, en formato video. Este material se centra en el fascinante mundo del emprendimiento educativo y destaca las increíbles experiencias y proyectos de varios participantes en la residencia de la Cátedra Unesco Movimiento Educativo Abierto para América Latina. Imagina que estamos explorando juntos cómo estos proyectos están transformando la educación, aportando innovaciones y soluciones que realmente marcan la diferencia. Este video no solo te permitirá conocer estas historias inspiradoras, sino que también te motivará a ver cómo tú mismo puedes contribuir al desarrollo educativo. Únete a esta comunidad de aprendizaje y descubramos juntos el impacto positivo que podemos generar. ¡Vamos a aprender construyendo!

REA: TecnoEmprendimiento- Soluciones de base tecnológica para los objetivos de desarrollo sostenible.
Autor: Jhonattan Miranda Mendoza.
Referencia: Miranda Mendoza, J. (2024). *TecnoEmprendimiento- Soluciones de base tecnológica para los objetivos de desarrollo sostenible* [Video]. https://hdl.handle.net/11285/676169

Compartimos un emocionante recurso educativo, en formato video, que no te puedes perder. Este video presenta un taller fascinante centrado en el emprendimiento tecnológico y la implementación de la Educación 4.0. Juntos, vamos a descubrir cómo las nuevas tecnologías pueden integrarse en la educación para mejorar el aprendizaje y fomentar la innovación. A través de ejemplos prácticos y discusiones enriquecedoras, este taller nos ofrece estrategias valiosas para todos aquellos que desean emprender en el sector educativo. Imagínate que estamos en este taller, aprendiendo y colaborando, compartiendo ideas y soluciones. Únete a esta comunidad de aprendizaje y descubramos juntos cómo podemos transformar la educación con tecnología. ¡Vamos a innovar juntos!

REA: Construyendo entornos diversos, abiertos y para todos: La educación del futuro.
Autores: Inés Álvarez-Icaza y Adolfo Rodríguez.
Referencia: Álvarez-Icaza, I. y Rodríguez, A. (2024). *Construyendo entornos diversos, abiertos y para todos: La educación del futuro* [Video]. Programa de webcast: Futuro de la educación en la complejidad. Tecnológico de Monterrey. https://hdl.handle.net/11285/676177

Compartimos un recurso educativo, en formato vídeo, que te hará sentir parte de una comunidad dedicada a la educación del futuro. Imagina que estamos juntos, construyendo entornos diversos, abiertos y accesibles para todos. Este video tiene como objetivo mostrar y recopilar estrategias que nos ayudarán a crear recursos educativos inclusivos y accesibles para todos. A través de esta experiencia compartida, aprenderemos cómo diseñar materiales que lleguen a más personas y fomenten una educación más equitativa. Únete a esta aventura y descubramos juntos cómo podemos contribuir a un futuro educativo más inclusivo. ¡Vamos a aprender como comunidad!

REA: Explorando el Potencial de la IA en la Evaluación de Competencias.
Autores: Jorge Carlos Sanabria Zepeda y Pamela Geraldine Olivo Montaño.
Referencia: Sanabria Zepeda, J.C. y Olivo Montaño, P.G. (2024). *Explorando el Potencial de la IA en la Evaluación de Competencias* [Video]. Programa de webcast: Futuro de la educación en la complejidad. Tecnológico de Monterrey. https://hdl.handle.net/11285/651643

▶ Proyectamos un recurso educativo, en formato video, que promete abrir nuevas puertas en el campo de la educación. Imagina que estamos juntos enfrentando un gran reto: medir el pensamiento complejo y descubrir cómo la inteligencia artificial (IA) puede automatizar este proceso. Este tema puede parecer controversial porque la IA sustituiría el rol tradicional del instructor en la evaluación. En este vídeo, te presentamos un caso de estudio fascinante sobre una plataforma impulsada por IA utilizada en el Ideatón CxT, junto con los primeros resultados de esta innovadora aplicación del proyecto Challenge OpenEDR4C. Acompáñame en esta aventura educativa para entender cómo la tecnología puede transformar nuestras metodologías de enseñanza y evaluación. ¡Vamos a evolucionar juntos!

REA: Adaptive Evaluation for Barriers Elimination: The OpenEDR4C Platform.
Autores: Inés Álvarez Icaza Longoria, José Martín Molina Espinosa, Paloma Suárez Brito e Ignacio Alvarado Reyes.
Referencia: Álvarez-Icaza, I., Suárez-Brito, P. y Molina-Espinosa, J. M., (2024) Adaptive Evaluation for Barriers Elimination: The OpenEDR4C Platform [Texto]. 12th International Conference on Information and Education Technology (ICIET 2024) <https://doi.org/10.1109/ICIET60671.2024.10542786 https://hdl.handle.net/11285/653803>.

▶ En un recurso educativo fascinante, presentado en un congreso internacional, se aborda un desafío crucial en nuestros tiempos: reducir la brecha digital y educativa entre estudiantes marginados y aquellos que aprenden a lo largo de toda su vida, en el contexto de los paradigmas de la Industria y Educación 4.0. En este texto, se explica cómo el aprendizaje adaptativo se ha convertido en una estrategia clave para aumentar la participación de los estudiantes, promoviendo la inclusión, la equidad y mejores resultados educativos. El estudio nos presenta tres valiosas contribuciones: una herramienta para conceptualizar plataformas inclusivas y accesibles, un marco para perfiles de aprendizaje adaptativo y la identificación de clases de usuarios basados en sus necesidades y características. Acompáñame en esta experiencia de aprendizaje y descubramos juntos cómo esta plataforma puede transformar la educación digital y hacerla accesible para todos. ¡Vamos a crecer en comunidad!

LLAMADO A LA ACCIÓN

¡Tu voz y tus ideas son cruciales para construir un futuro mejor juntos!
Los desafíos globales que enfrentamos requieren la colaboración y el aprovechamiento de la diversidad de pensamientos y habilidades. Por eso, te invitamos a unirte a nosotros en esta misión. Ya sea que tengas proyectos innovadores, investigaciones en curso, ideas que quieras llevar a la práctica o un deseo de capacitar a tu comunidad, queremos trabajar contigo. Desde la sociedad civil, las escuelas, las universidades, hasta las empresas y los grupos legislativos, cada sector tiene una perspectiva única que puede enriquecer nuestro enfoque. Ayúdanos a impulsar el pensamiento complejo y el emprendimiento social, científico y tecnológico.

¡Vamos a crear juntos un futuro lleno de oportunidades y soluciones sostenibles!
Nuestro grupo de investigación: https://tec.mx/es/r4c-irg
Explora nuestros proyectos: https://www.research4challenges.world/

Únete al proyecto Plataforma OpenEdR4C:
https://www.research4challenges.world/openedr4c

GLOSARIO

Educación 5.0. Una forma de educación que se apoya en la tecnología para facilitar experiencias personalizadas, enriquecidas con recursos didácticos y estrategias activas para facilitar el aprendizaje y la atención a la diversidad. Se vincula con las demandas del mercado laboral en las capacidades digitales, la automatización y la inteligencia artificial para potenciar la productividad y el bienestar humano.

Emprendimiento científico. Proceso que contiene la aplicación de conocimientos y descubrimientos científicos para la creación de nuevas empresas o productos innovadores y disruptivos, que resuelvan retos y /o necesidades, ya sea de una comunidad o de una empresa. Este proceso significa la identificación de oportunidades comerciales basadas en la investigación científica y el desarrollo tecnológico.

Emprendimiento social. Se enfoca en crear, evaluar y perseguir oportunidades que transformen positivamente a las comunidades y los sistemas productivos, además de valor económico. Este tipo de emprendimiento valora la sostenibilidad ambiental y social, y se centra en apoyar a los agentes de cambio que están comprometidos con la misión de la empresa social. En pocas palabras, se trata de negocios que no solo ganan dinero, sino que también generan un impacto positivo y duradero en la sociedad.

Emprendimiento tecnológico. Proceso de creación, desarrollo y gestión de empresas o proyectos que utilizan la tecnología de manera innovadora para ofrecer productos o servicios disruptivos en el mercado. Además, el emprendimiento tecnológico implica identificar oportunidades de negocios intensivos en tecnología, reunir recursos y gestionar un crecimiento y riesgo significativo. Esta definición subraya cómo el emprendimiento tecnológico se diferencia de otros tipos de emprendimiento, centrándose en la tecnología como núcleo de la nueva empresa o en la incorporación sustancial de nuevas tecnologías en la operación o diseño del proyecto.

Objetivos de Desarrollo Sostenible (ODS). Los ODS son un conjunto de metas globales y concretas orientadas a la acción, cuyo propósito es proteger el planeta, erradicar la pobreza y alcanzar la paz y la prosperidad para todas las personas. Cada ODS incluye diversas metas específicas que detallan cómo lograr cada objetivo, promoviendo un enfoque integral para el desarrollo sostenible en todo el mundo.

Pensamiento complejo. El pensamiento complejo es la competencia de observar la realidad considerando la totalidad de los factores que convergen para darle forma. En lugar de enfocarse en cada factor de manera aislada, se entiende que cada parte contribuye y es influida por la totalidad de la realidad. Este enfoque integrador permite comprender cómo las diferentes partes se interrelacionan y afectan mutuamente, proporcionando una visión más completa y profunda del mundo.

Futuro de la Educación – Future of Education

Edited by María Soledad Ramírez-Montoya, Rasikh Tariq, Leonardo David Glasserman Morales, Edgar Omar López-Caudana & Inés Alvarez-Icaza Longoria

VOL. 1 María Soledad Ramírez-Montoya, Edgar Omar López-Caudana, Inés Alvarez-Icaza Longoria, Carlos Vásquez-Parra, Fabian Eduardo Basabe, Carolina Alcántar-Nieblas, Pamela Geraldine Olivo Montaño, Virginia Rodés Paragarino, Isolda Margarita Castillo-Martínez, Laura Icela González-Pérez & May Portuguez Castro: Mobilise Your Thinking for Complexity. Open Educational Model for Complex Thinking – Moviliza tu Pensamiento para la Complejidad. Modelo Educativo Abierto para el Pensamiento Complejo. 2026.

VOL. 2 María Soledad Ramírez-Montoya, Edgar Omar López-Caudana, Inés Alvarez-Icaza Longoria, Carlos Enrique George Reyes, Paloma Suárez Brito & Pamela Geraldine Olivo Montaño: Education 5.0 to mobilise social, scientific and technological entrepreneurship. OpenEdR4C Platform – Educación 5.0 para movilizar emprendimiento social, científico y tecnológico. Plataforma OpenEdR4C. 2026.

www.peterlang.com

Zeitfracht Medien GmbH
Ferdinand-Jühlke-Straße 7
99095 Erfurt, Deutschland
produktsicherheit@kolibri360.de

Druck:
CPI Druckdienstleistungen GmbH
im Auftrag der
Zeitfracht Medien GmbH
Ein Unternehmen der Zeitfracht - Gruppe
Ferdinand-Jühlke-Str. 7
99095 Erfurt